# Maths Matters

Edco

# Contents

# Introduction

**Maths Matters 5** has been devised and developed by two very experienced primary teachers and comprehensively emcompasses all the objectives and recommendations of the Revised Mathematics Primary School Curriculum. The revised curriculum is presented in the form of five different strands — Number, Algebra, Shape and Space, Measures, and Data. The strands are colour-coded in **Maths Matters 5** for ease of use (see Contents for colours). These strands, although presented in separate sections, are not treated in isolation but are developed as integrated units in which ideas in one area are supportive of ideas and concepts dealt with in other strands.

While the area of Number is treated with due importance, this is not at the expense of the other strands, which receive a much greater emphasis than heretofore, as recommended in the revised curriculum.

## The key features of this book include:

- Development of new topics in **carefully graded and systematic steps**.

- Revision and consolidation of the salient features of the Fourth Class programme in the **Looking Back** sections at the beginning of each chapter.

- Revision and review sections are included at regular intervals throughout the book in the **Time to Look Back** sections, to assess the pupils' progress through the Fifth Class programme.

- A handy **You need** list at the beginning of each chapter to assist the teacher in the preparation of manipulatives and the introduction of new concepts and terminology.

- Entertaining **activity-based exercises** at the end of most chapters, which help to revise and consolidate key areas of the preceding chapter.

- Emphasis on readily available concrete materials and **manipulatives**.

- Increased stress on discussion, estimation and problem solving in **real-life, child-centred situations**. Many opportunities are provided for the pupils to apply their mathematical understanding in contexts drawn from their own experiences and environments.

- The use of **high quality full colour** throughout will greatly assist in the development of a positive attitude among the pupils towards mathematics.

**You need:**
- a calculator
- to revise multiplication facts
- to revise long multiplication
- numeral cards 0-9

I'm sure your brain is a little bit rusty and slow after the summer holidays, so here are a few questions to oil the creaky parts and loosen up the muscles after the long break.

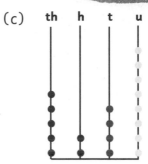

1. Write the numbers shown on these abacuses.

(a) 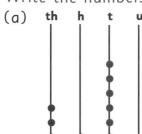  (b) 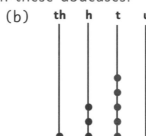  (c)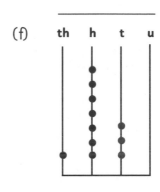

_____   _____   _____

(d) 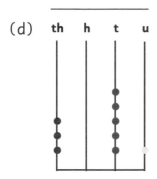  (e) 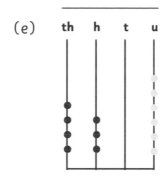  (f)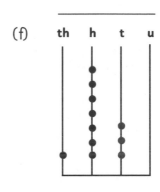

_____   _____   _____

(g) Put the above 6 numbers in order beginning with the smallest.

_____, _____, _____, _____, _____, _____,

2. Show these 4 numbers on the abacuses below.

(a) 4065   (b) 3058   (c) 5320   (d) 6004

| th | h | t | u |
|---|---|---|---|

| th | h | t | u |
|---|---|---|---|

| th | h | t | u |
|---|---|---|---|

| th | h | t | u |
|---|---|---|---|

3. Write the value of the 7 in each of these numbers.

(a) 3798 _____   (b) 4007 _____   (c) 8574 _____   (d) 7034 _____

# Looking back – addition

1. Find the answers to these questions in your head.

   (a) Add 36 and 24. _____

   Isn't it nice to be back?

   (b) Find the sum of 88 and 12. _____

   (c) John spent 48c on a packet of sweets and 29c on a bar.
   How much did he spend? _____

   (d) What number is 16 bigger than 44? _____

   (e) By how much is 100 bigger than 72? _____

   (f) Paul has 68c but Niamh has 39c more than him. How much has Niamh? _____

   (g) Find the total cost of these three items. _____

2. Find the sum of these numbers.

   (a) 36, 574, 1394 and 9 = _____        (b) 3954, 804, 8 and 72 = _____

3. Try these in your copy.

   (a) 376 + 574 = _____      (b) 814 + 295 = _____      (c) 916 + 207 = _____

   (d) 848 + 96 = _____      (e) 1247 + 643 = _____      (f) 7041 + 984 = _____

   (g) 848 + 1764 + 9 = _____    (h) 6474 + 8 + 248 = _____    (i) 67 + 191 + 8004 = _____

4. Now try these in your copy.

   (a) 5296 + 864 + 7 + 1906 = _____        (b) 8 + 7032 + 96 + 865 = _____

   (c) 794 + 17 + 3704 + 860 = _____        (d) 954 + 8674 + 19 + 8 = _____

   (e) 9001 + 69 + 340 + 9 = _____        (f) 8240 + 6 + 759 + 85 = _____

# Looking back – calculator time

Try this on your calculator, but first estimate your answer.

3864 + 841 + 79

Estimate: 3900 + 800 + 80 = 4780.

Exact answer on calculator is   `3 8 6 4 + 8 4 1 + 7 9 = 4 7 8 4`

1.  Now try these using your calculator. Estimate first.
    (a) 4972 + 703 + 42          Estimate: _____   Exact answer: _____
    (b) 1864 + 694 + 59          Estimate: _____   Exact answer: _____
    (c) 3742 + 74 + 6 + 921      Estimate: _____   Exact answer: _____
    (d) 31 + 901 + 1731 + 9      Estimate: _____   Exact answer: _____

2.  Do these in your head.

    (a) What is the difference between 22 and 40? _____

    (b) By how much is 16 smaller than 50? _____

    (c) John is 9 years old and his Dad is 41 years old.
        How much older is Dad? _____

    (d) Take 23 from 100. _____

    (e) Paula had 60c. She spent 42c.
        How much had she left? _____

3.  Now try these.

    (a) 86 – 14 = _____   (b) 79 – 16 = _____   (c) 69 – 36 = _____

    (d) 80 – 15 = _____   (e) 91 – 14 = _____   (f) 85 – 37 = _____

    (g)   324      (h)   427      (i)   694      (j)   795      (k)   952
        – 161          – 134          – 292          – 197          – 376
        ─────          ─────          ─────          ─────          ─────

    (l)   321      (m)   432      (n)   901      (o)   730      (p)   900
        – 168          – 169          – 467          – 369          – 534
        ─────          ─────          ─────          ─────          ─────

4.  (a) 3701 – 896 = _____      (b) 4670 – 984 = _____      (c) 7006 – 878 = _____

    (d) 9032 – 1674 = _____     (e) 3709 – 748 = _____      (f) 8000 – 904 = _____

# Problems for you to solve

1. In an election Mary O'Brien got 3746 votes, and Miriam Murphy got 4931 votes.
   (a) Who got the most votes? _____

   (b) How many more votes did she get? _____

2. Take 365 from the sum of 867 and 392. _____

3. There were 8500 people at a football match. There were 4268 men, 2674 women and the remainder were children.

   (a) How many children were at the match? _____

   (b) How many more men than women? _____

   (c) How many less childen than adults? _____

4. What must be added to 1836 to make 5041? _____

5. Using the following 4 digits: 4, 3, 7, 2,

   (a) make the largest possible number _____   (b) make the smallest possible number _____

   (c) find the sum of those 2 numbers _____

   (d) find the difference between the 2 numbers _____

6. Neil Armstrong was the first person to set foot on the moon in 1969. How many years ago is that? _____

7. You can use your calculator to find the answer to these problems.

   (a) By how much is 9800 greater than the sum of 386, 5792 and 1706? _____

   (b) By how much is the sum of 2644 and 6938 greater than the sum of 7946 and 845? _____

   (c) Increase 7032 by 939. _____

4

# Looking back – multiplication

1. Try these.

| (a) 36 | (b) 48 | (c) 56 | (d) 72 | (e) 84 | (f) 38 |
|---|---|---|---|---|---|
| x 2 | x 3 | x 4 | x 6 | x 5 | x 7 |

| (g) 59 | (h) 48 | (i) 96 | (j) 72 | (k) 49 | (l) 74 |
|---|---|---|---|---|---|
| x 9 | x 8 | x 4 | x 6 | x 5 | x 7 |

2. Now try these.

| (a) 249 | (b) 394 | (c) 467 | (d) 896 | (e) 284 | (f) 314 |
|---|---|---|---|---|---|
| x 6 | x 4 | x 3 | x 5 | x 7 | x 8 |

3. Do these long multiplication sums in your copy.

| (a) 36 | (b) 84 | (c) 96 | (d) 88 | (e) 72 | (f) 48 |
|---|---|---|---|---|---|
| x 10 | x 10 | x 20 | x 40 | x 50 | x 70 |

| (g) 35 | (h) 48 | (i) 74 | (j) 96 | (k) 76 | (l) 98 |
|---|---|---|---|---|---|
| x 14 | x 16 | x 18 | x 25 | x 32 | x 45 |

| (m) 65 | (n) 72 | (o) 58 | (p) 98 | (q) 86 | (r) 35 |
|---|---|---|---|---|---|
| x 49 | x 64 | x 37 | x 32 | x 74 | x 28 |

## Problems for you to solve

1. Michael treated his 6 friends to a meal in a fast food restaurant on his 10th birthday. Each meal cost €4.95. How much did he have to pay? _____

2. There are 32 children in fifth class in Jamestown School. Mrs Brown, their teacher, collected €18 from each pupil to go on a school trip. How much did she collect altogether? _____

3. A school bus can hold 36 children. How many children would fit on 18 buses? _____

# Moving on – bigger numbers

How is the brain working now?
I hope it is a lot fitter than it was when you started this chapter.

Are you ready for bigger numbers?

Example:

| 2 | 7 | 4 | 9 | 5 |

This is the number of miles on the clock of Ms Foley's car after a year's driving.
**Now look at that number on an abacus picture.**

5 = 5 miles

9 = 90 miles

4 = 400 miles

7 = 7000 miles

2 = 2 x 10 000 = 20 000 miles

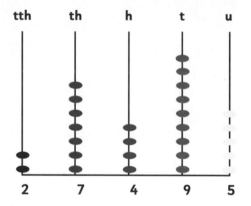

1.  Write the number on the abacus in words.

_____

2.  Which digit is worth the most? _____

Yes, 2 is the digit that is worth the most because 2 stands for 2 ten thousands, which is 20 000.

3.  Which digit is worth the least? _____

4.  Very soon Ms Foley's car will have thirty thousand miles on the clock.

Show that number on this abacus picture.

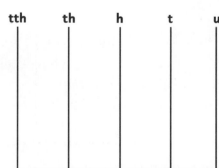

# Bigger numbers

1.  Look at this number:  7 9 8 6 4

That is the number of people who attended the All-Ireland Football Final in Croke Park. Write the number in words.

_____

Now write the value of the

(a) 7 = _____

(b) 9 = _____

(c) 8 = _____

(d) 6 = _____

(e) 4 = _____

(f) Using these five digits make the biggest number possible. _____

(g) Using these five digits make the smallest number possible. _____

2. Write these numbers. The first one is done for you.

(a) Sixty-four thousand, three hundred and fifty-two = **64 352**

(b) Thirty-six thousand, eight hundred and ninety-three = _____

(c) Seventy-two thousand, nine hundred and sixteen = _____

(d) Now show these three big numbers on these abacus pictures

(i)

| tth | th | h | t | u |
|-----|-----|-----|-----|-----|

_____

(ii)

| tth | th | h | t | u |
|-----|-----|-----|-----|-----|

_____

(iii)

| tth | th | h | t | u |
|-----|-----|-----|-----|-----|

_____

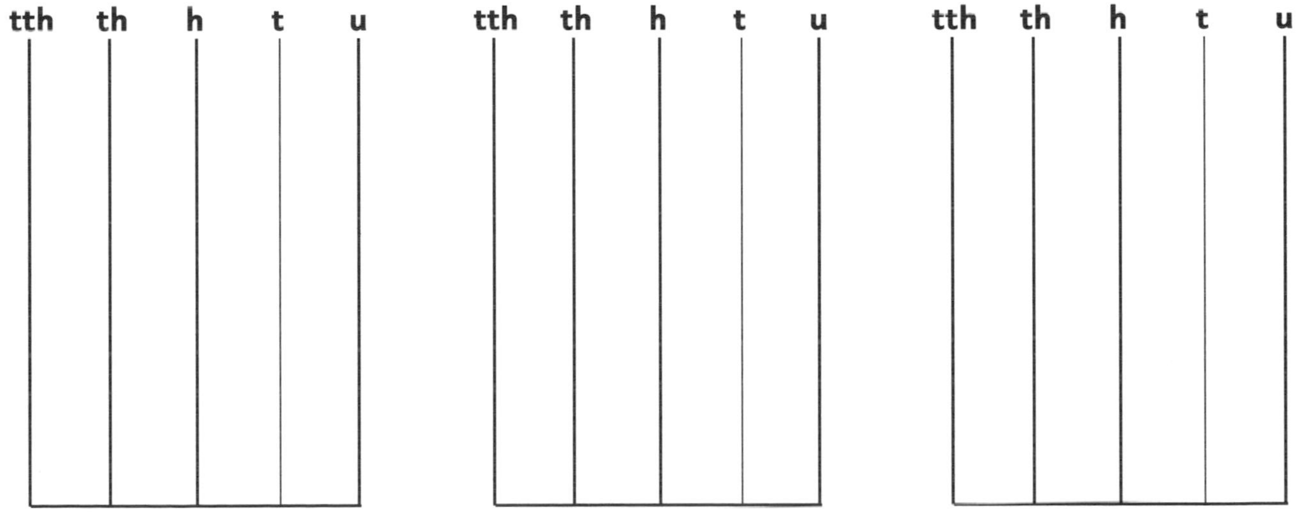

# Bigger numbers

Try these.

(a)  18 294 + 7960 + 84 = _____

(b)  968 + 7 + 12 364 = _____

(c)  7384 + 12 042 + 68 = _____

(d)  29 364 + 18 + 7302 = _____

(e)  18 704 − 9876 = _____

(f)  82 314 − 18 465 = _____

(g)  42 107 − 6739 = _____

(h)  61 290 − 18 308 = _____

● Check all your answers using a calculator.

# Know your place!

Here is a game for you to play with your friends.

1.  You need 4 players.

2.  You need 10 cards with a different digit
    on each: 0, 1, 2, 3, 4, 5, 6, 7, 8, 9.
    The cards are placed face down on the desk.

3.  Each player draws a table like this in their
    mathematics copy or on a piece of paper.

4.  Choose a game leader. The leader picks one of
    the cards and each player writes the digit in
    any box of their table.
    The game leader picks 5 cards in all.

5.  The player who has built the greatest
    number is the winner.

6.  The teacher can play this game with the
    whole class as well.

7.  Now – just to change the rules, the
    winner can be the person who makes
    the smallest number.

By the way, a number cannot
begin with 0.

# Chapter 2
## Lines and Angles

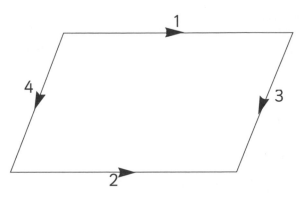

**You need:**
- a ruler
- a set square
- a clock face
- colouring pencils

## A    Looking back

Look at this shape.

Side 1 is parallel to Side 2.

Side 3 is parallel to Side 4.

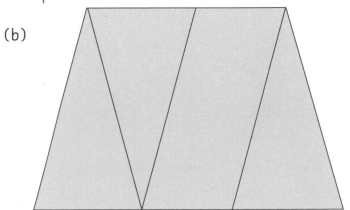

1. Draw arrows to show the parallel lines in these shapes.

(a)

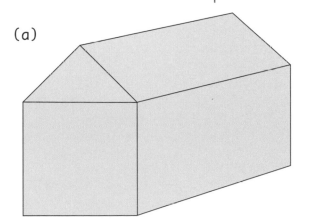

(b)

2. Make a list of 3 places in the classroom where you can see parallel lines and then draw one of them in the box.

   (a) _____

   (b) _____

   (c) _____

3. True or False?

|  | True | False |
|---|---|---|
| (a) A railway line has parallel lines. | ☐ | ☐ |
| (b) A semi-circle has 2 parallel lines. | ☐ | ☐ |
| (c) Parallel lines will never intersect. | ☐ | ☐ |
| (d) There are no parallel lines in this shape:  | ☐ | ☐ |
| (e) The double yellow lines on a road are parallel. | ☐ | ☐ |

# More looking back

1. Unscramble these letters to make 3 words, which describe lines.

   (a) tloiohrzna               (b) lairvtec              (c) auinperlcderp

       h_____               v_____            p_____

   Do you know what the 3 words mean?_____

2. Here is a shape that has horizontal and vertical lines.

   Mark 1 on the horizontal lines and 2 on the vertical lines.

   (a) There are _____ horizontal lines.          (b) There are _____ vertical lines.

When a vertical line and a horizontal line meet they are said to be **perpendicular**.
Line A is perpendicular to Line B.
This symbol ⊥ means 'perpendicular to'.   A ⊥ B

                                                     A

                                                     B

3. Look at this rectangle. Can you see the lines that are perpendicular?

                 1

                                  Fill in the missing numbers.

                                  Line 1 ⊥ Lines **2** and **4** .

  4                           2    Line 4 ⊥ Lines \_\_\_\_ and \_\_\_\_.

                                  Line 3 ⊥ Lines \_\_\_\_ and \_\_\_\_.

                                  Line 2 ⊥ Lines \_\_\_\_ and \_\_\_\_.

                 3

4. Now with your ruler and your set square,

   (a) draw a horizontal line here and mark it 1.

   (b) draw a line perpendicular to that line and mark it 2.

   (c) draw another line perpendicular to line 1 and mark it 3.

   (d) How many vertical lines can you see? _____ What are their numbers? _____

   (e) How many parallel lines can you see? _____ What are their numbers? _____

# Angles

## B Looking back

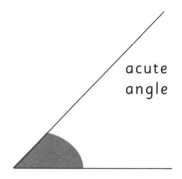

right
angle

A right angle
is a corner.

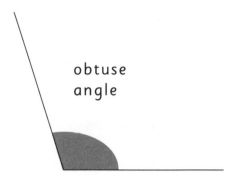

acute
angle

An acute angle
is smaller than a corner.

obtuse
angle

An obtuse angle
is bigger than a corner.

1. Look at these shapes. Mark 1 where you see a right angle,
   2 for an acute angle and 3 for an obtuse angle.

(a)

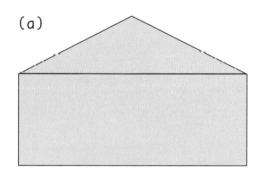

(b)

(c)

(d)

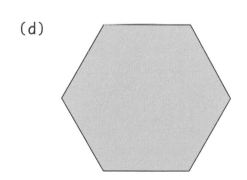

(e) How many of each angle are there?

(i) Right _____          (ii) Acute _____          (iii) Obtuse _____

# More angles

1. Draw the hands on these clock faces to show the times written underneath.
   Then say what kind of angle is between the hands.

(a)

Three o'clock

_____angle

(b)

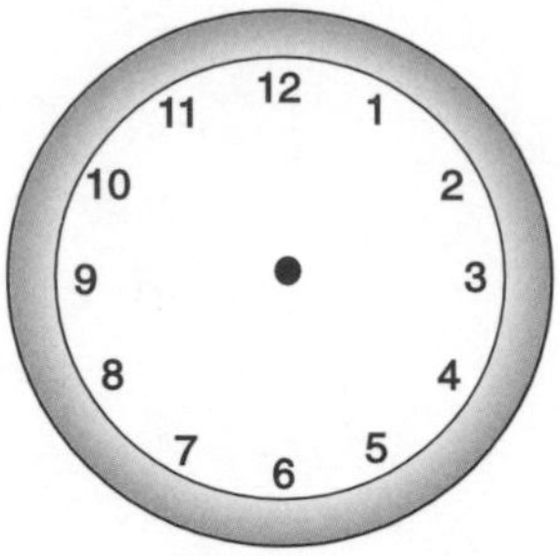

Quarter past one

_____angle

(c)

Half past ten

_____angle

(d)

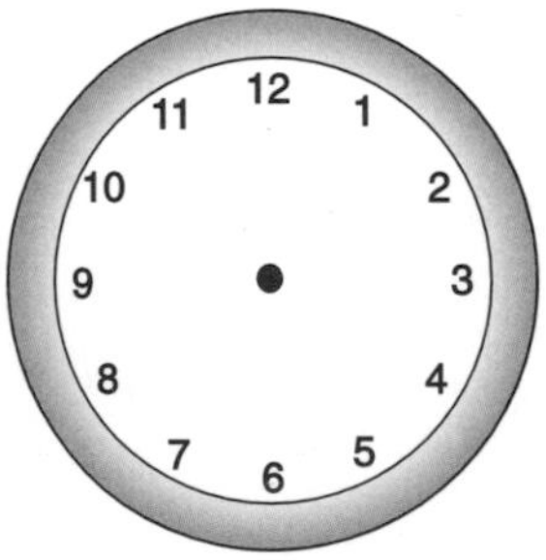

Nine o'clock

_____angle

(e)

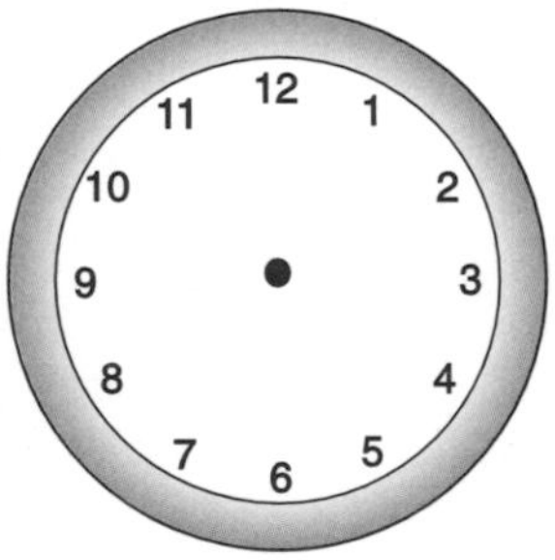

Five to twelve

_____angle

(f)

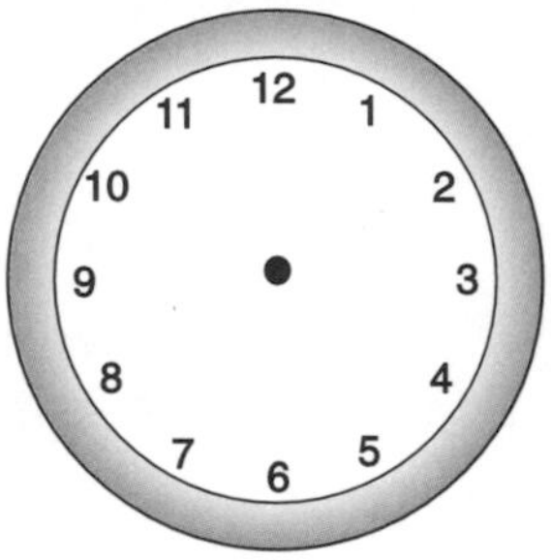

Ten to six

_____angle

2. Look at these capital letters. Mark 1 for right angles, 2 for acute angles
   and 3 for obtuse angles.

(a)

(b)

(c)

Now draw three other capital letters that do not have curved lines and mark the angles
in the same way.

(d)

(e)

(f)

# Moving on – reflex angles

An angle is a rotation.

The teacher will get the class clock face and show it to the class.

- First of all the teacher will show 12 o'clock on the face.

  What kind of an angle is between the hands?
  Yes, you're right. There is no angle.

- Then the teacher will show ten past twelve.
  That is an _____ angle.

- Now the teacher will rotate the hands to show:

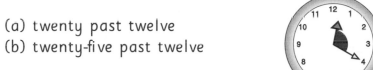

(a) twenty past twelve
(b) twenty-five past twelve

What kind of angle is shown at (a) _____ (b) _____ ?

At 6 o'clock the angle between the hands is called a **straight angle**.

- Now the teacher will rotate the hands to show **twenty-five to one.**

  The angle between the hands is now bigger than
  a straight angle.

  Have you any idea what we call this kind of an angle? _____

- Now the teacher will show
  (a)  twenty to one
  (b)  a quarter to one
  (c)  ten to one
  (d)  five to one

The angles formed at (a), (b), (c) and (d) are _____ angles.

When the minute hand is rotated to show one o'clock, the minute hand has
now done one **full turn** or **rotation**.

# Reflex angles

1. Colour the reflex angles in these shapes in red.

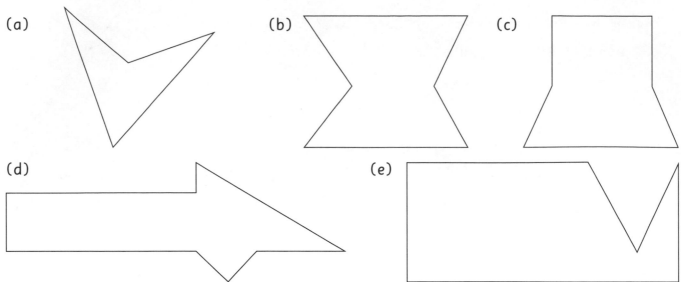

(a)

(b)

(c)

(d)

(e)

2. Draw a shape with a reflex angle in each of these boxes.
   Colour the reflex angles in red.

(a)

(b)

(c)

3. Describe the angles between the hands on these clock faces.
   The first one is done for you.

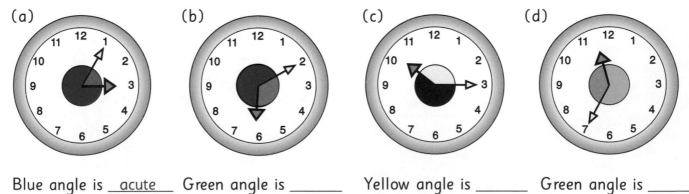

(a)

Blue angle is __acute__

Red angle is __reflex__

(b)

Green angle is _____

Red angle is _____

(c)

Yellow angle is _____

Black angle is _____

(d)

Green angle is _____

Pink angle is _____

# Time to flex your muscles

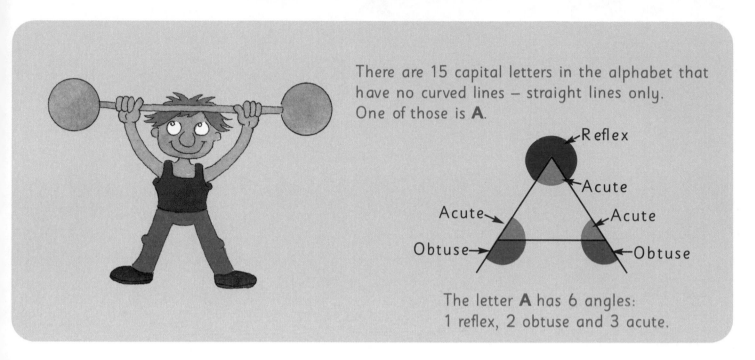

There are 15 capital letters in the alphabet that have no curved lines – straight lines only. One of those is **A**.

Reflex
Acute
Acute
Acute
Obtuse
Obtuse

The letter **A** has 6 angles: 1 reflex, 2 obtuse and 3 acute.

Draw 8 other capital letters that have reflex angles. Draw them in the boxes below and colour the reflex angles in red.

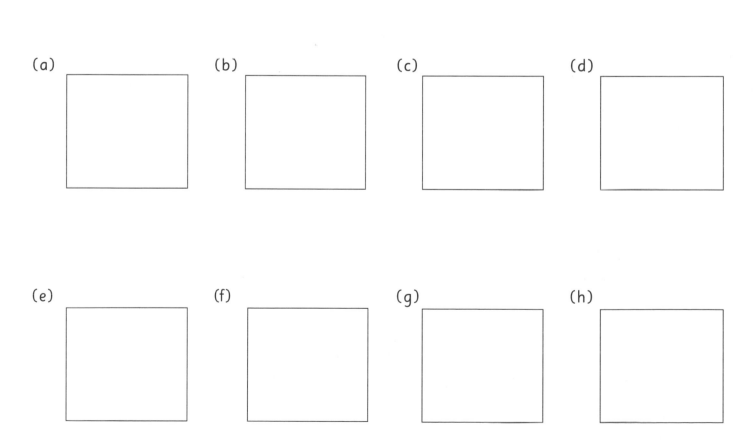

(a)

(b)

(c)

(d)

(e)

(f)

(g)

(h)

# Chapter 3
## Money

**You need:**
– a calculator
– euro coins and notes
– to revise 'averages'

There are 12 countries using the euro currency.
Ireland, of course, is one of them.
How many of the other countries can you name? _____
Write them in your copy.

1. There are 8 coins and 7 notes. The coins are:

____    ____    ____    ____    ____    ____    ____    ____

and the notes are:

____    ____    ____    ____    ____    ____    ____

2. What coins would you use to buy these?

(a) Magazine
€1.59

(b) Football
€1.95

(c) Packet of 12 markers
€1.99

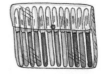

_____        _____        _____

3. What is the least amount of coins you would use to buy these?

(a)  Bar of chocolate
79c

(b)  Fountain pen
€1.29

(c)  Ice cream cone
86c

**50c +** _____        _____        _____

(d)  Football magazine
€2.35

(e)  Maths set
€3.64

(f)  Packet of
10 copybooks
€4.99

_____        _____        _____

# Shop bills

When you buy several items from a shop, setting out a bill helps you to find the total cost and the change you should get.

**Look at this example:**

| Ball €1.95 | Skateboard €10.99 | Book €5.25 | Pencil 26c |
|---|---|---|---|

| Ball: | €1.95 | €20.00 |
|---|---|---|
| Skateboard: | €10.99 | − €18.45 |
| Book: | €5.25 | €1.55 |
| Pencil: | + €0.26 | |
| Total cost: | €18.45 | |

Change out of €20 = €1.55.

In your copy set out bills and find the change when the following items are bought. The amount of money handled is shown opposite the items:

| CD €8.95 | Kite €6.50 | Hamburger €1.85 |
|---|---|---|

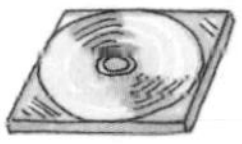

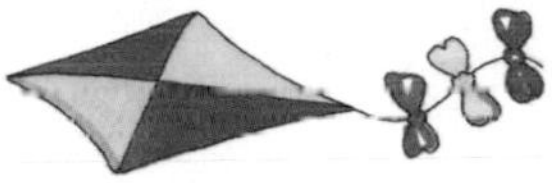

| Drink 95c | T-Shirt €7.99 | Cinema Ticket €4.50 |
|---|---|---|

(a) CD and a drink — €10

(b) Drink and hamburger — €5

(c) Cinema ticket and T-shirt — €15

(d) Cinema ticket and hamburger — €7

(e) Drink and cinema ticket — €10

(f) Kite and T-shirt — €20

(g) CD, hamburger and drink — €15

(h) Cinema ticket, kite and T-shirt — €20

(i) CD, T-shirt and kite — €25

(j) Drink, hamburger and cinema ticket — €8

Using your calculator, find the total cost of the 6 items and your change out of €35.

Cost: _____   Change: _____

17

# More bills

Mrs Brown sent her son, Michael, to the shop to get the following:

3 litres of milk at €1.09 a litre

2 loaves of bread at 96c a loaf

6 apples at 38c each

What change did Michael get out of €10?

| | €1.09 | €0.96 | €0.38 | €3.27 | €10.00 |
|---|---|---|---|---|---|
| | x 3 | x 2 | x 6 | €1.92 | – €7.47 |
| | €3.27 | €1.92 | €2.28 | + €2.28 | |

Total Cost: €7.47    Change: €2.53

1. In your copy set out the following bills and then find the correct change out of the money handed in.

   (a) 5 pencils @ 19c each and 5 biros @ 38c each:  €4

   (b) 2 plastic rulers @ 37c each and 4 pencil sharpeners @ 29c each:  €2

   (c) 5 oranges @ 28c each and 8 scones @ 32c each:  €4

   (d) 2 computer games @ €6.45 each and 3 videos @ €8.49 each:  €40

   (e) 3 pairs of socks @ €2.99 each and 4 ties @ €5.95 each:  €35

2. Use your calculator to find out whether Mrs Green or Mrs Black gets the better value.
   (a) Mrs Green did her shopping in 'SUPERKING'S'
   (b) Mrs Black went shopping at 'SUPERQUEEN'S'

| No. | Item | Each | |
|---|---|---|---|
| 3 | Milk | 60c | |
| 5 | Apples | 26c | |
| 3 | Peaches | 28c | |
| 4 | Cabbage | 49c | |
| **Total Cost:** | | | |

| No. | Item | Each | |
|---|---|---|---|
| 3 | Milk | 58c | |
| 5 | Apples | 28c | |
| 3 | Peaches | 32c | |
| 4 | Cabbage | 47c | |
| **Total Cost:** | | | |

# Problems for you to solve

1. Martina wants to buy a skateboard for €21.50.
   She has €16.95. How much more does she need? _____

2. Plastic rulers cost 48c.
   What is the cost of 36 rulers? _____

3. Five maths books cost €52.50.
   How much would 9 books cost? _____

4.  The local supermarket had a special offer on white
   bread rolls. You could buy a pack of 6 for €1.39 or
   buy them singly at 28c each.
   How much would you save if you
   bought a pack of 6? _____

5. John and Jennifer were picking apples for Farmer O'Brien last summer.
   They worked 6 days a week from 10.00 am to 6.00 pm at €5.50 an hour.
   How much did each earn in a week? _____

6. Tennis balls cost 60c each. How many balls can
   Portnoo Tennis Club buy for €20.00 _____ and
   how much change will be left over? _____

7. Gabrielle and Michael were saving for their summer
   holiday trip to Italy. Gabrielle saved €33.50 but
   Michael saved €7.95 more than her. How much
   did they save altogether between them? _____

# Euro crossword

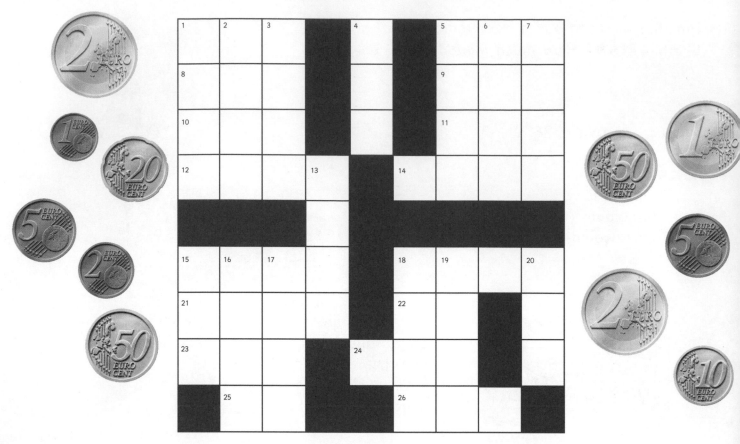

## Across

1. €2.49 + €1.67 = _____
5. €6.46 − €2.97 = _____
8. €1.79 x 5 = _____
9. €76.56 ÷ 8 = _____
10. 9 apples @ 27c each = _____
11. €32.64 ÷ 6 = _____
12. Difference between €60 and €4.78 = _____
14. €20.00 − €5.32 = _____
15. 3 CDs @ €9.50 each = _____
18. $\frac{1}{4}$ of €75 = _____
21. Two cent more than €20 = _____
22. Take €5.00 from €100. _____
23. 47c more than €2.50 = _____
24. Change from €50 after spending €48.29 = _____
25. 19 times 5c = _____
26. 9 tickets for €3.60. How much for 6 tickets? _____

## Down

1. Tom won €100. He spent €51.75. How much had he left? _____
2. 55c less than €20 = _____
3. €6.32 more than €59 = _____
4. 9 oranges for €2.25. How much for 5? _____
5. €6.59 x 6 = _____
6. €60 − €14.54 = _____
7. €24.37 x 4 = _____
13. The year we started using euro coins and notes. _____
15. 6 copybooks @ 37c each = _____
16. 1c less than €81 = _____
17. €50 increased by 75c = _____
18. €20 − 28c = _____
19. €9.46 x 9 = _____
20. $\frac{1}{8}$ of a €4,000 prize = _____

# All in a day's work

1. David is attending a post-primary (or second level) school but he has a part-time job at the weekend working in a supermarket.

   (a) Last Saturday he worked for 8 hours and earned €46.00. How much does he earn per hour? _____

   (b) On Sunday he worked for 5 hours. How much did he earn on Sunday? _____

   (c) How much did he earn altogether for the weekend? _____

   (d) He paid €4.50 in tax. How much did he bring home with him? _____

   Do these using your calculator.

2. The manager of the Grand Hotel offered David's big sister, Martina, a permanent job working in the restaurant. For a 40-hour week she would earn €250. But Martina only wanted to work part-time for 15 hours a week.

   (a) How much would she earn per hour? _____

   (b) How much would she earn per week? _____

3. Garda Michael Ryan's take-home pay is €300 for a 40-hour week.

   (a) How much does he earn per hour? _____

   (b) How much would he earn in 6 weeks? _____

   (c) Week 1:     38 hours     _____

   (d) Week 2:     33 hours     _____

   (e) Week 3:     46 hours     _____

   (f) Week 4:     51 hours     _____

   (g) Week 5:     48 hours     _____

   (h) Week 6:     43 hours     _____

   (i) Total earned in these 6 weeks:     _____

   (j) Average weekly earnings:     _____

# Chapter 4
## Long Division

**You need:**
– to devote a lot of time to oral work on page 22
– to do the examples on the board also
– to explain 'product'

1. Do these questions in your head and then write the answers.

   (a) How many 10's in 70? _____

   (b) How many 10's in 90? _____

   (c) How many 12's in 36? _____

   (d) How many 12's in 60? _____

   (e) How many 11's in 77? _____

   (f) How many 11's in 99? _____

   (g) How many 13's in 39? _____

   (h) How many 13's in 65? _____

   (i) How many 20's in 100? _____

   (j) How many 20's in 120? _____

   (k) How many 20's in 160? _____

   (l) How many 20's in 200? _____

   (m) Share 180 sweets among 20 children. _____

   (n) How many 20's in 180? _____

   (o) Divide 144 children into 12 equal groups. _____

   (p) How many 12's in 144? _____

   (q) How many times can you take 25 out of 300? _____

   (r) How many 25's in 300? _____

   (s) Divide 140 sweets among 14 children. _____

   (t) How many 14's in 140? _____

2. Now write the answers to these questions.

   (a) Divide 130 by 13. _____

   (b) How many 13's in 130? _____

   (c) How many 15's in 150? _____

   (d) Divide 150 by 15. _____

   (e) How many 18's in 180? _____

   (f) Divide 180 by 18. _____

   (g) Divide €150 among 15 people. How much does each get? _____

   (h) How many 15's in 150? _____

   (i) How many 16's in 160? _____

   (j) Divide €160 among 16 people. _____

   What did you notice about each answer?_____

   Yes, the answer is ___ for all the questions. Keep this in mind when you are trying to work out the answers to more difficult division questions.

# Long division made easy

**Example 1:** How many 13's in 143? You write it like this: 143 ÷13.

Break up the 143 into 2 parts: 130 + 13
Now, how many 13's in 130?    __10__
How many 13's in 13?  __1__
So, altogether there are eleven 13's in 132.

Now you see how easy long division can be!

**Short way:**
$$\begin{array}{r} 10+\ 1 \\ 13\ \overline{|\ 130+13} \end{array}$$

**Answer:** __11__

---

**Example 2:** How many 14's in 168? You write it like this: 168 ÷14.

Break up the 168 into 2 parts: 140 + 28
Now, how many 14's in 140?    __10__
How many 14's in 28?    __2__
So, altogether there are twelve 14's in 168.

No problem to you!

**Short way:**
$$\begin{array}{r} 10+\ 2 \\ 14\ \overline{|\ 140+28} \end{array}$$

**Answer:** __12__

---

**Example 3:** How many 15's in 195? You write it like this: 195 ÷ 15.

Break up the 195 into 2 parts: 150 + 45
How many 15's in 150?    __10__
How many 15's in 45?    __3__
So, altogether there are thirteen 15's in 195.

How many 15's in 195?

_____

Well done!

**Short way:**
$$\begin{array}{r} 10+\ 3 \\ 15\ \overline{|\ 150+45} \end{array}$$

**Answer:** __13__

# Long division – over to you

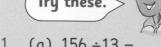

Try these.

1.  (a)  156 ÷13 =

         13 | 10+ 2
            | 130+26          Answer: __12__

    (b)  182 ÷14 =

         14 | 140+42          Answer:_____

    (c)  180 ÷15 =

         15 |    +            Answer:_____

    (d)  176 ÷16 =

         16 |                 Answer:_____

    (e)  208 ÷16 =

         16 |                 Answer:_____

    (f)  221 ÷17 =

            |                 Answer:_____

    (g)  255 ÷17 =

            |                 Answer:_____

    (h)  234 ÷18 =

            |                 Answer:_____

    (i)  209 ÷19 =

            |                 Answer:_____

    (j)  247 ÷19 =

            |                 Answer:_____

These questions are a little more difficult.

2.  (a)  273 ÷13 =

         13 | 20+ 1
            | 260+13          Answer: __21__

    (b)  294 ÷14 =

         14 | 280+14          Answer:_____

    (c)  330 ÷15 =

         15 | 300+30          Answer:_____

    (d)  368 ÷16 =

         16 |                 Answer:_____

    (e)  391 ÷17 =

         17 |                 Answer:_____

    (f)  425 ÷17 =

         17 |                 Answer:_____

# Bigger numbers

As the numbers get bigger we need to learn a shorter way of doing long division. Here are 3 examples to help you.

## Example 1

Divide 195 by 13.

195 ÷ 13

```
        15
  13 ) 195
      -13↓
        65
       -65
         0
```

Answer: **15**

This means that there are fifteen 13's in 195.

### Step 1
Find out how many 13's in 19.
Yes, there is one 13 in 19.
So put 1 in the answer slot.

### Step 2
Take the 13 from the 19 and there is 6 left. Now take down the 5 beside the 6. Now you have 65.

### Step 3
How many 13's in 65?
Yes, there are 5 with no remainder because 5 x 13 = 65.
The answer is 15.

## Example 2

Divide 240 children into 15 groups.
How many children in each group?

240 ÷ 15

```
        16
  15 ) 240
      -15↓
        90
       -90
        00
```

Answer: **16**

This means that there are 16 in each group.

### Step 1
Find out how many 15's in 24.
Yes, there is one 15 in 24.
Put 1 in the answer slot.

### Step 2
Take 15 from 24 and there is 9 left over. Now take down the 0 beside the 9. Now you have 90.

### Step 3
How many 15's in 90?
There are 6 with no remainder because 6 x 15 = 90.
The answer is 16.

## Example 3 Try this one on your own using the short method.

15 cans of orange drink can fit into a box. How many boxes are needed for 375 cans?

```
  15 ) 375
      ___

      ___
```

Answer: _____ boxes are needed to hold 375 cans of orange.

# Long division – over to you again

Keep up the good work!

1. Try these on your own in your copy.

   (a) 368 ÷ 16     (b) 425 ÷ 17     (c) 468 ÷ 18     (d) 420 ÷ 15

   (e) 406 ÷ 14     (f) 437 ÷ 19     (g) 338 ÷ 13     (h) 493 ÷ 17

   (i) 552 ÷ 24     (j) 624 ÷ 26     (k) 667 ÷ 23     (l) 756 ÷ 28

2. Now try these. They are a little more difficult.

   (a) 837 ÷ 31     (b) 627 ÷ 33     (c) 988 ÷ 38     (d) 980 ÷ 35

   (e) 966 ÷ 42     (f) 855 ÷ 45     (g) 987 ÷ 47     (h) 931 ÷ 49

   (i) 867 ÷ 51     (j) 848 ÷ 53     (k) 960 ÷ 60     (l) 992 ÷ 62

# Problems for you to solve

1. There are 405 pupils in Greenfield National School. The Principal, Ms Robinson, divided them into groups of 15. How many groups were there? _____

2. There are 16 biscuits in a packet of biscuits. How many packets can be made with 576 biscuits? _____

3. 990 supporters from Donegal travelled to Dublin by bus for the All-Ireland Football Final. Each bus could hold 45 people. How many buses were needed to carry the supporters? _____

4. When 16 is multiplied by another number the product is 432. Find the other number. _____

   16 x ? = 432

5. In the factory, scissors are packed in boxes of 24. How many boxes are needed to supply an order of 840 scissors to a big arts and crafts shop? _____

26

# The School Concert

The teachers and the pupils of St Patrick's School organised a concert last year. There were two performances as the hall was not big enough to hold all the people who wanted to see the show.

Can you find the answers to the following questions?

1. The school collected
   • €1830 worth of adult tickets,
   • €280 worth of children's tickets and
   • €840 worth of family tickets.

   (a) How many adults attended the concert? _____

   (b) How many children attended? _____

   (c) How many families were at the concert? _____

   (d) How much money was collected altogether? _____

   (e) It cost €765 to organise the concert. How much profit did the school make on the concert? _____

2. They sold 280 books of tickets at the interval. It cost €275 to provide the prizes.

   How much profit did the school make on the raffle? _____

3. After the concert many people stayed back to sample something from the food and drinks menu provided by the Parents' Association.

   They sold:
   (a) 72 cups of tea = _____    (b) 80 cups of coffee = _____

   (c) 48 scones = _____    (d) 24 slices of apple tart = _____

   (e) They collected €18.00 for minerals.
   How many minerals did they sell? _____

   (f) They collected €9.20 on crisps.

   How many packets did they sell? _____

   (g) What was the total takings on food and drink? _____

   (h) It cost €75 to provide the food and drink.

   How much profit did they make on food and drink? _____

4. Total profit on concert, raffle and food and drink = €_____

---

**Admission fee**

Adults     €6

Children   €4

Family     €15
(2 Adults  2 children)

**Raffle**

Tickets: Book of 6 €5

---

**MENU**

Tea ..... 60 c

Coffee.... 75 c

Scones.... 40 c each

Apple tart ... €1 50 per slice

Minerals .... 75 c

Crisps..... 40 c

# Chapter 5

## Time to look back 1

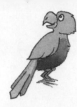

1. Put these five numbers in order beginning with the largest.

374 8746 73 7 16 247

________ ________ ________ ________ ________

2. Add these five numbers:

96 + 16 242 + 795 + 7359 + 9 = __________

3. Find the sum of these numbers:

948 + 7312 + 74 = __________

4. 6204 – 1576 = __________

5. 8001 – 764 = __________

6. Find the difference between 796 and 904. ______

7. 268 x 7 = ______

8. €3.95 x 9 = ______

9. 76 x 48 = ______

10. How many 16's are in 192? ______

11. 180 ÷ 15 ______

12. 442 ÷ 17 = ______

13. 575 ÷ 23 = ______

14. Look at the 4 angles marked A, B, C and D. Shade in the acute angle.

**A**

**B**

**C**

**D**

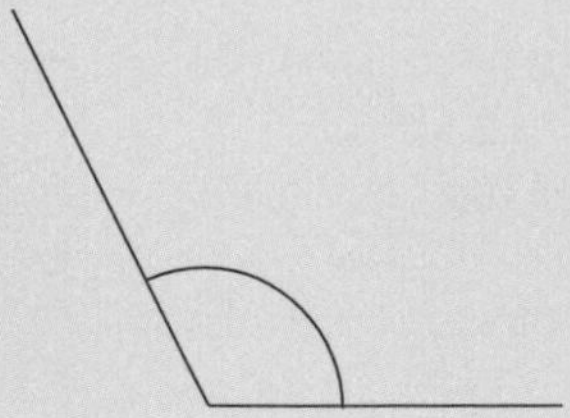

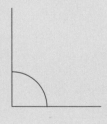

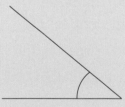

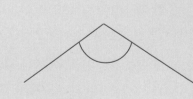

# Time to look back 1

15. Only one of these statements is true.
Put a tick (✓) in the box beside the correct one.

(a) Line 1 is perpendicular to Line 9. ☐

(b) Line 1 is parallel to Line 8. ☐

(c) Line 3 is horizontal. ☐

(d) Line 4 is vertical. ☐

(e) Line 2 is perpendicular to Line 10. ☐

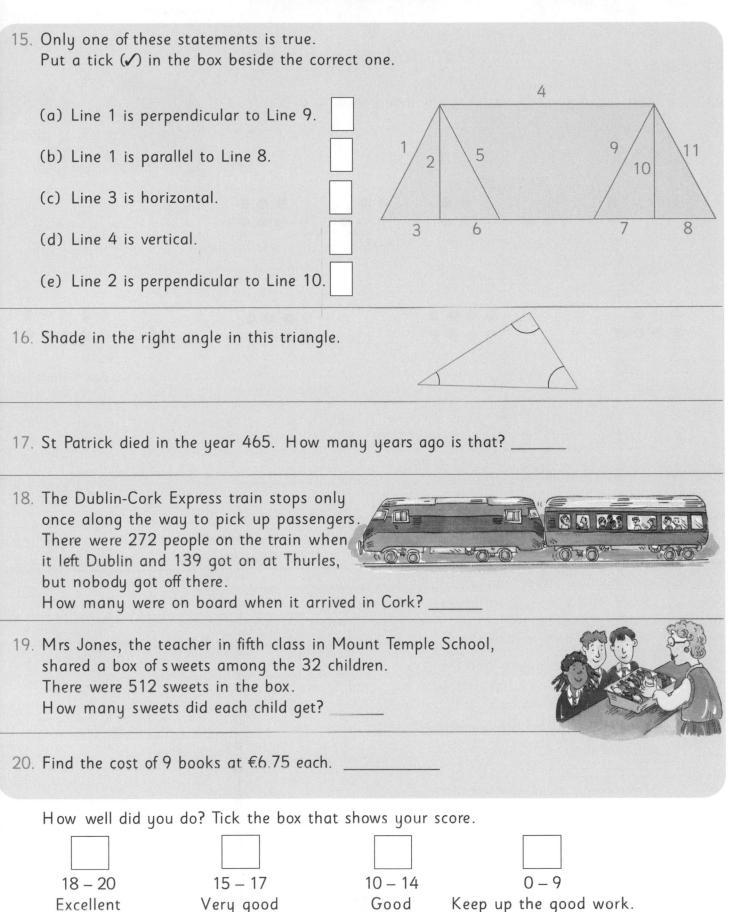

16. Shade in the right angle in this triangle.

17. St Patrick died in the year 465. How many years ago is that? _____

18. The Dublin-Cork Express train stops only once along the way to pick up passengers. There were 272 people on the train when it left Dublin and 139 got on at Thurles, but nobody got off there.
How many were on board when it arrived in Cork? _____

19. Mrs Jones, the teacher in fifth class in Mount Temple School, shared a box of sweets among the 32 children.
There were 512 sweets in the box.
How many sweets did each child get? _____

20. Find the cost of 9 books at €6.75 each. _____

How well did you do? Tick the box that shows your score.

| ☐ | ☐ | ☐ | ☐ |
|---|---|---|---|
| 18 – 20 | 15 – 17 | 10 – 14 | 0 – 9 |
| Excellent | Very good | Good | Keep up the good work. |

29

You need:
- to explain 'consecutive'
- colouring pencils

## Odd and even numbers

1. Look at these dot pictures of the numbers from 1 to 10.

1    2    3    4    5    6

7    8    9    10

Some of these numbers make **even** shapes.

Write those 5 numbers: _____, _____, _____, _____, _____
These are called __ __ __ n numbers.

The other 5 numbers make **odd** shapes.

Write those 5 numbers: _____, _____ , _____, _____, _____.
These are called __ __ d numbers.

2. (a) Write in all the even numbers on
      this 100 square and then colour them red.

  (b) Now write in the odd numbers
      and colour them blue.

  (c) How many even numbers in
      the 100 square? _____

  (d) How many odd numbers? _____

  (e) Discuss the patterns you see with a friend.

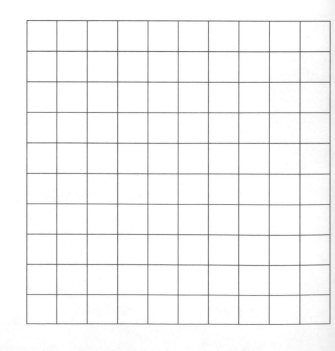

# Odd and even numbers

1. All even numbers end in **0**, or _____, or _____, or _____, or _____.

   All odd numbers end in **1**, or _____, or _____, or _____, or _____.

   When you divide an even number by 2 there is no re__ __ __ __ __ __ __ __.

   There is always a remainder of _____ when you divide an odd number by 2.

In your copy practise dividing odd and even numbers by 2.

2. (a) Circle the even numbers:

   16,    21,    19,    8,    7,    12,    24,    38,    50,    1,    98,    99

   (b) Circle the odd numbers:

   13,    22,    11,    17,    25,    34,    41,    60,    75,    82

2 + 3 = 5
Even plus odd = odd.

5 + 3 = 8
Odd plus odd = even.

3. Fill in the missing words 'odd' or 'even'.

   (a) odd + odd = _____         (b) even + even = _____

   (c) even + _____ = odd         (d) odd + _____ = even

   (e) odd + even + odd = _____   (f) odd + odd + odd = _____

   (g) even + odd + _____ = even  (h) even + even + even = _____

   (i) _____ + odd + even + odd = odd   (j) odd − even = _____

4. (a) Write 10 even numbers that end in 4.

   ____,    ____,    ____,    ____,    ____,    ____,    ____,    ____,    ____,    ____.

   (b) Write 10 odd numbers that end in 9.

   ____,    ____,    ____,    ____,    ____,    ____,    ____,    ____,    ____,    ____.

# Square numbers

Look at these pictures of the number 4 and the number 9.

4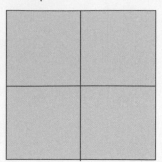

9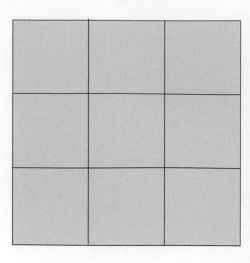

The numbers 4 and 9 are called square numbers
because they make the shape of a square.

● 4 is the first square number.   ● 9 is the second square number.

What is the next square number? _____
Draw a picture in your copy.

1. Fill in the missing words.

   (a) The first square number is _____

   (b) The second square number is _____

   (c) Find the missing numbers in the sequence: 4, 9, 16, ____, ____, ____, ____, ____, ____.

   (d) Draw a hundred square in your copy and colour in all the square numbers.

   (e) Discuss the pattern they make with another child.

   (f) How many square numbers less than 100 are there? _____

Now look at this:

| | |
|---|---|
| 1 + 3 = | 4 |
| 1 + 3 + 5 = | 9 |

Discuss what you noticed with your teacher and class.

2. (a) When you add the first two _____ numbers you get the first _____ number.

   (b) When you add the first _____ odd numbers you get the _____ square number.

   (c) What number do you get when you add the first 4 consecutive odd numbers? _____

# Rectangular numbers

|    |  |  |  |  |  |  |    |  |  |  |  |  |  |  |
|----|--|--|--|--|--|--|----|--|--|--|--|--|--|--|
| 2  |  |  |  |  |  |  | 8  |  |  |  |  |  |  |  |
|    |  |  |  |  |  |  |    |  |  |  |  |  |  |  |
| 3  |  |  |  |  |  |  |    |  |  |  |  |  |  |  |
|    |  |  |  |  |  |  | 10 |  |  |  |  |  |  |  |
| 5  |  |  |  |  |  |  |    |  |  |  |  |  |  |  |
|    |  |  |  |  |  |  |    |  |  |  |  |  |  |  |
| 6  |  |  |  |  |  |  | 12 |  |  |  |  |  |  |  |
|    |  |  |  |  |  |  |    |  |  |  |  |  |  |  |

Look at the grid above. The number of squares that shows each number has been coloured in.

All of those numbers make a rectangular shape.

They are called **r**___ ___ ___ ___ ___ ___ ___ ___ ___ ___ numbers.

1. On the grid below draw and colour the rectangular shapes of these numbers.
   Use a different colour for each number.

   (a) 7        (b) 11        (c) 14        (d) 15        (e) 20

# More rectangular numbers

1. Some numbers can have more than one rectangular shape.
   For example, the number 6 can be drawn in 2 different ways:

   **6**

   **6**

   (a) Now find the next 3 numbers that can have more than one
       rectangular shape. _____, _____, _____
   (b) Draw the rectangles for these numbers in this grid.

   **Remember! A square is a special kind of a rectangle.**

2. The number 12 has 3 rectangular shapes.

   **12**

   **12**

   **12**

   Colour in these shapes in different colours.
   (a) Now find another number that can have 3 rectangular shapes. _____
       Draw these shapes in your copy.
   (b) Can you find a number that has 4 rectangular shapes? _____
   (c) Draw the 4 rectangles in your copy.

# Chapter 7

## Fractions 1

**You need:**
- A4 sheets of paper
- colouring pencils
- to revise symbols < and >
- to explain 'equivalence' and 'simplest form'

## A    Looking back

1.  Rearrange these letters to find three words similar in meaning to
    the word **fraction**.

    (a) ptar _____    (b) hreas _____    (c) cipee _____

2.  Write these fractions.

    (a) two thirds  [—]      (b) nine tenths  [—]      (c) five sixths  [—]

    (d) seven eighths  [—]    (e) three quarters  [—]    (f) eleven twelfths  [—]

3.  Fill in the missing numbers in these fractions.

    $$1 = \frac{2}{2} = \frac{3}{3} = \frac{\phantom{0}}{4} = \frac{\phantom{0}}{5} = \frac{\phantom{0}}{6} = \frac{\phantom{0}}{8} = \frac{\phantom{0}}{9} = \frac{\phantom{0}}{10} = \frac{\phantom{0}}{12}$$

4.  Colour the amounts shown.

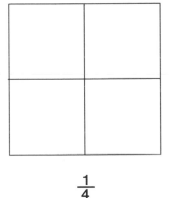

$$\frac{1}{4}$$

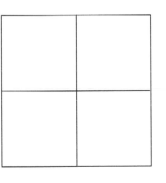

$$\frac{3}{4}$$

$$\frac{2}{3}$$

5.  What fraction of each shape is coloured?

    (a)                                     (b)                     (c)

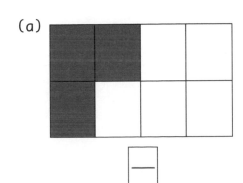

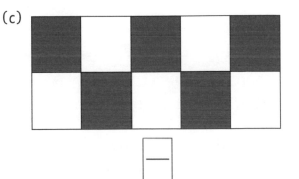

[—]                          [—]                          [—]

# Looking back again

1. Now find

   (a) $\frac{5}{8}$ of 72 _____

   (b) $\frac{7}{9}$ of 18 _____

   (c) $\frac{7}{10}$ of 80 _____

   (d) $\frac{5}{6}$ of 48 _____

   (e) $\frac{3}{4}$ of 36 _____

   (f) $\frac{3}{5}$ of 45 _____

   Use your calculator to check your answers.

Example: _____ is $\frac{1}{3}$ of 18   18 ÷ 3 = 6,   so  6 is $\frac{1}{3}$ of 18.

2. Now try these.

   (a) _____ is $\frac{1}{4}$ of 24

   (b) _____ is $\frac{1}{9}$ of 27

   (c) _____ is $\frac{1}{10}$ of 100

This is $\frac{3}{10}$ of Áine's money.   How much money has she?

$\frac{3}{10}$ = 60c          $\frac{1}{10}$ = 60c ÷ 3 = 20c          $\frac{10}{10}$ = 10 x 20c = 200c = €2

3. Now find the full amount if

   (a) $\frac{2}{5}$ = 20 _____

   (b) $\frac{7}{8}$ = 63 _____

   (c) $\frac{3}{4}$ = 18 _____

   (d) $\frac{5}{6}$ = 45 _____

| One Unit | | | | | | | | | | | |
|---|---|---|---|---|---|---|---|---|---|---|---|
| $\frac{1}{2}$ | | | | | | $\frac{1}{2}$ | | | | | |
| $\frac{1}{3}$ | | | | $\frac{1}{3}$ | | | | $\frac{1}{3}$ | | | |
| $\frac{1}{4}$ | | | $\frac{1}{4}$ | | | $\frac{1}{4}$ | | | $\frac{1}{4}$ | | |
| $\frac{1}{5}$ | | $\frac{1}{5}$ | | $\frac{1}{5}$ | | $\frac{1}{5}$ | | $\frac{1}{5}$ | | | |
| $\frac{1}{6}$ | | $\frac{1}{6}$ | | $\frac{1}{6}$ | | $\frac{1}{6}$ | | $\frac{1}{6}$ | | $\frac{1}{6}$ | |
| $\frac{1}{7}$ | $\frac{1}{7}$ | | $\frac{1}{7}$ | | $\frac{1}{7}$ | | $\frac{1}{7}$ | | $\frac{1}{7}$ | | $\frac{1}{7}$ |
| $\frac{1}{8}$ | $\frac{1}{8}$ | $\frac{1}{8}$ | | $\frac{1}{8}$ | | $\frac{1}{8}$ | | $\frac{1}{8}$ | | $\frac{1}{8}$ | $\frac{1}{8}$ |
| $\frac{1}{9}$ | $\frac{1}{9}$ | $\frac{1}{9}$ | $\frac{1}{9}$ | | $\frac{1}{9}$ | | $\frac{1}{9}$ | | $\frac{1}{9}$ | $\frac{1}{9}$ | $\frac{1}{9}$ |
| $\frac{1}{10}$ | $\frac{1}{10}$ | $\frac{1}{10}$ | $\frac{1}{10}$ | $\frac{1}{10}$ | $\frac{1}{10}$ | | $\frac{1}{10}$ | $\frac{1}{10}$ | $\frac{1}{10}$ | $\frac{1}{10}$ | $\frac{1}{10}$ |
| $\frac{1}{11}$ | $\frac{1}{11}$ | $\frac{1}{11}$ | $\frac{1}{11}$ | $\frac{1}{11}$ | $\frac{1}{11}$ | $\frac{1}{11}$ | $\frac{1}{11}$ | $\frac{1}{11}$ | $\frac{1}{11}$ | $\frac{1}{11}$ | $\frac{1}{11}$ |
| $\frac{1}{12}$ | $\frac{1}{12}$ | $\frac{1}{12}$ | $\frac{1}{12}$ | $\frac{1}{12}$ | $\frac{1}{12}$ | $\frac{1}{12}$ | $\frac{1}{12}$ | $\frac{1}{12}$ | $\frac{1}{12}$ | $\frac{1}{12}$ | $\frac{1}{12}$ |

4. Use your fraction wall to fill in the missing numbers in these fractions.

   (a) $\frac{1}{2}$ = $\frac{}{4}$

   (b) $\frac{2}{3}$ = $\frac{}{9}$

   (c) $\frac{1}{4}$ = $\frac{}{12}$

   (d) $\frac{4}{5}$ = $\frac{8}{}$

   (e) $\frac{2}{6}$ = $\frac{}{3}$

# Still looking back

1. Put these fractions in the correct position on the number lines.

(a) $\frac{1}{2}$, $\frac{1}{4}$, $\frac{3}{4}$

(b) $\frac{1}{2}$, $\frac{1}{6}$, $\frac{5}{6}$, $\frac{2}{3}$

(c) $\frac{1}{10}$, $\frac{1}{2}$, $\frac{7}{10}$, $\frac{2}{5}$

# Problems for you to solve

1. There are 60 minutes in one hour. Michelle spent $\frac{3}{4}$ of an hour at her homework last night. How many minutes is that? _____

2.  There are 210 pages in Roald Dahl's book **'Going Solo'**. Darren read $\frac{2}{7}$ of the book last weekend. How many pages did he read? _____

3. There are 40 games for each team in the Premier League. When $\frac{5}{8}$ of the games were played Liverpool was 3 points ahead of the rest. How many games had Liverpool played at that stage? _____

4.  This oil tank holds 350 litres when it is full. Last winter the Woods family used $\frac{4}{5}$ of the oil. How many litres were left in the tank? _____

5. Jennifer spent $\frac{3}{8}$ of her money when she went on her school tour last year. She had €60 left.

(a) How much money did she have before she went on the tour? _____

(b) How much money did she spend on the day of the tour? _____

# Equivalence

## B Moving on

The word **'equivalent'** means **'of equal value'**.

  is **equivalent** to

60c                                                                60c

One hundred cent is **equivalent** to one euro.

1. Fold three A4 sheets of paper like this to show:

   2 halves                         4 quarters                        8 eighths

   Now you can see that $\frac{1}{2}$ is equivalent to $\frac{2}{4}$ and to $\frac{4}{8}$.     $\frac{1}{2} = \frac{2}{4} = \frac{4}{8}$

   (a) $\frac{1}{4} = \overline{8}$          (b) $\frac{3}{4} = \overline{8}$          (c) $1 = \overline{2} = \overline{4} = \overline{8}$

2. Fold four A4 sheets of paper like this to show:

   3 thirds             6 sixths             9 ninths             12 twelfths

   Now use your sheets to help you to fill in the missing numbers in the questions below.

   (a) $\frac{1}{3} = \overline{6} = \overline{9} = \overline{12}$     (b) $\frac{2}{3} = \overline{6} = \overline{9} = \overline{12}$     (c) $1 = \overline{3} = \overline{6} = \overline{9} = \overline{12}$

3. Fold two A4 sheets of paper like this to show 5 fifths and 10 tenths
   and fill in the missing numbers.

   (a) $\frac{1}{5} = \overline{10}$     (b) $\frac{2}{5} = \overline{10}$     (c) $\frac{3}{5} = \overline{10}$     (d) $\frac{4}{5} = \overline{10}$     (e) $1 = \overline{5} = \overline{10}$

38

# More equivalence

1. Use your folded sheets to complete these lists of equivalent fractions.

   (a) $\frac{1}{2}$ = $\frac{}{4}$ = $\frac{}{6}$ = $\frac{}{8}$ = $\frac{}{10}$ = $\frac{}{12}$  (b) $\frac{1}{4}$ = $\frac{}{8}$ = $\frac{}{12}$  (c) $\frac{2}{3}$ = $\frac{}{6}$ = $\frac{}{9}$ = $\frac{}{12}$

   (d) $\frac{2}{3}$ = $\frac{}{6}$ = $\frac{}{9}$  (e) 1 = $\frac{}{2}$ = $\frac{}{3}$ = $\frac{}{4}$ = $\frac{}{5}$ = $\frac{}{6}$ = $\frac{}{7}$ = $\frac{}{8}$ = $\frac{}{9}$ = $\frac{}{10}$ = $\frac{}{12}$

2. Look at your fraction wall and see if you can find any fractions equivalent to the fractions written here. Write **Yes** or **No** beside each one.

   (a) $\frac{1}{7}$ _____  (b) $\frac{2}{7}$ _____  (c) $\frac{3}{7}$ _____  (d) $\frac{4}{7}$ _____  (e) $\frac{5}{7}$ _____  (f) $\frac{6}{7}$ _____

3. Now check to see if there are any equivalent fractions for the elevenths.
   Write **Yes** or **No**.

   (a) $\frac{1}{11}$ _____  (b) $\frac{2}{11}$ _____  (c) $\frac{3}{11}$ _____  (d) $\frac{4}{11}$ _____  (e) $\frac{5}{11}$ _____

   (f) $\frac{6}{11}$ _____  (g) $\frac{7}{11}$ _____  (h) $\frac{8}{11}$ _____  (i) $\frac{9}{11}$ _____  (j) $\frac{10}{11}$ _____

4. (a) How many marbles can you see in each set below? _____

   (b) A fraction of each set is coloured red. Write that fraction under each set.

   (c) $\frac{1}{2}$ of 16 = _____    $\frac{2}{4}$ of 16 = _____    $\frac{4}{8}$ of 16 = _____    So $\frac{1}{2}$ = ☐ = ☐

   (d) $\frac{3}{4}$ of 16 = _____    $\frac{6}{8}$ of 16 = _____    So ☐ = ☐

5. (a) How many marbles in each set below? _____

   (b) A fraction of each set is coloured red. Write that fraction under each set.

   (c) $\frac{1}{3}$ of 27 = _____    $\frac{3}{9}$ of 27 = _____    So ☐ = ☐

   (d) $\frac{2}{3}$ of 27 = _____    $\frac{6}{9}$ of 27 = _____    So ☐ = ☐

# Equivalence – once more

1. Here are 2 sets of marbles with 12 in each set.

   **Set 1** ○ ○ ○ ○ ○ ○        **Set 2** ○ ○ ○ ○ ○ ○
              ○ ○ ○ ○ ○ ○                          ○ ○ ○ ○ ○ ○

   (a) Colour $\frac{1}{6}$ of the first set in red.      (b) Colour $\frac{1}{12}$ of the second set in red.

   (c) $\frac{1}{6}$ of 12 = _____        $\frac{2}{12}$ of 12 = _____    So $\boxed{\frac{\phantom{x}}{\phantom{x}}}$ = $\boxed{\frac{\phantom{x}}{\phantom{x}}}$

   (d) $\frac{2}{6}$ of 12 = _____        $\frac{4}{12}$ of 12 = _____    So $\boxed{\frac{\phantom{x}}{\phantom{x}}}$ = $\boxed{\frac{\phantom{x}}{\phantom{x}}}$

   (e) $\frac{3}{6}$ of 12 = _____        $\frac{6}{12}$ of 12 = _____    So $\boxed{\frac{\phantom{x}}{\phantom{x}}}$ = $\boxed{\frac{\phantom{x}}{\phantom{x}}}$

   (f) $\frac{4}{6}$ of 12 = _____        $\frac{8}{12}$ of 12 = _____    So $\boxed{\frac{\phantom{x}}{\phantom{x}}}$ = $\boxed{\frac{\phantom{x}}{\phantom{x}}}$

   (g) $\frac{5}{6}$ of 12 = _____        $\frac{10}{12}$ of 12 = _____    So $\boxed{\frac{\phantom{x}}{\phantom{x}}}$ = $\boxed{\frac{\phantom{x}}{\phantom{x}}}$

2. In your copy draw two sets of marbles with 10 marbles in each.
   Put 2 lines of 5 marbles in each set.

   (a) Colour $\frac{1}{5}$ of the first set in red.      (b) Colour $\frac{1}{10}$ of the second set in red.

   (c) $\frac{1}{5}$ of 10 = _____        $\frac{2}{10}$ of 10 = _____    So $\boxed{\frac{\phantom{x}}{\phantom{x}}}$ = $\boxed{\frac{\phantom{x}}{\phantom{x}}}$

   (d) $\frac{2}{5}$ of 10 = _____        $\frac{4}{10}$ of 10 = _____    So $\boxed{\frac{\phantom{x}}{\phantom{x}}}$ = $\boxed{\frac{\phantom{x}}{\phantom{x}}}$

   (e) $\frac{3}{5}$ of 10 = _____        $\frac{6}{10}$ of 10 = _____    So $\boxed{\frac{\phantom{x}}{\phantom{x}}}$ = $\boxed{\frac{\phantom{x}}{\phantom{x}}}$

   (f) $\frac{4}{5}$ of 10 = _____        $\frac{8}{10}$ of 10 = _____    So $\boxed{\frac{\phantom{x}}{\phantom{x}}}$ = $\boxed{\frac{\phantom{x}}{\phantom{x}}}$

3. Use the fraction wall to help you to fill in the equivalent fractions in these lists.

   (a) $\frac{1}{2}$ = $\boxed{\frac{\phantom{x}}{\phantom{x}}}$ = $\boxed{\frac{\phantom{x}}{\phantom{x}}}$ = $\boxed{\frac{\phantom{x}}{\phantom{x}}}$ = $\boxed{\frac{\phantom{x}}{\phantom{x}}}$ = $\boxed{\frac{\phantom{x}}{\phantom{x}}}$      (b) $\frac{1}{3}$ = $\boxed{\frac{\phantom{x}}{\phantom{x}}}$ = $\boxed{\frac{\phantom{x}}{\phantom{x}}}$ = $\boxed{\frac{\phantom{x}}{\phantom{x}}}$

   (c) $\frac{2}{3}$ = $\boxed{\frac{\phantom{x}}{\phantom{x}}}$ = $\boxed{\frac{\phantom{x}}{\phantom{x}}}$ = $\boxed{\frac{\phantom{x}}{\phantom{x}}}$      (d) $\frac{1}{4}$ = $\boxed{\frac{\phantom{x}}{\phantom{x}}}$ = $\boxed{\frac{\phantom{x}}{\phantom{x}}}$ = $\boxed{\frac{\phantom{x}}{\phantom{x}}}$      (e) $\frac{3}{4}$ = $\boxed{\frac{\phantom{x}}{\phantom{x}}}$ = $\boxed{\frac{\phantom{x}}{\phantom{x}}}$ = $\boxed{\frac{\phantom{x}}{\phantom{x}}}$

   (f) $\frac{1}{5}$ = $\boxed{\frac{\phantom{x}}{\phantom{x}}}$      (g) $\frac{2}{5}$ = $\boxed{\frac{\phantom{x}}{\phantom{x}}}$      (h) $\frac{3}{5}$ = $\boxed{\frac{\phantom{x}}{\phantom{x}}}$      (i) $\frac{4}{5}$ = $\boxed{\frac{\phantom{x}}{\phantom{x}}}$

   > **< less than**
   > **> greater than**

4. Put the correct sign **>**, **=** or **<** between these sets of fractions.

   (a) $\frac{1}{2}$    $\frac{2}{4}$    (b) $\frac{7}{8}$    $\frac{3}{8}$    (c) $\frac{2}{5}$    $\frac{4}{5}$    (d) $\frac{5}{9}$    $\frac{2}{9}$    (e) $\frac{3}{7}$    $\frac{5}{7}$

   (f) $\frac{4}{5}$    $\frac{7}{10}$    (g) $\frac{5}{10}$    $\frac{1}{2}$    (h) $\frac{2}{3}$    $\frac{5}{6}$    (i) $\frac{6}{8}$    $\frac{3}{4}$    (j) $\frac{7}{8}$    $\frac{1}{8}$

   (k) $\frac{2}{3}$    $\frac{3}{4}$    (l) $\frac{6}{8}$    $\frac{1}{4}$    (m) $\frac{3}{12}$    $\frac{1}{4}$    (n) $\frac{9}{10}$    $\frac{4}{5}$    (o) $\frac{2}{3}$    $\frac{1}{6}$

# Simplest form

You can find equivalent fractions by multiplying the number above the line and the number below the line by the same number.

You know that $\frac{1}{2} = \frac{2}{4} = \frac{4}{8}$
by multiplying $\frac{1^{\times 2}}{2^{\times 2}} = \frac{2}{4}$

and $\frac{2^{\times 2}}{4^{\times 2}} = \frac{4}{8}$

So $\frac{1}{2} = \frac{2}{4} = \frac{4}{8}$

But $\frac{1}{2}$ is the **simplest form**

You know that $\frac{1}{3} = \frac{2}{6} = \frac{4}{12}$
by multiplying $\frac{1^{\times 2}}{3^{\times 2}} = \frac{2}{6}$

and $\frac{2^{\times 2}}{6^{\times 2}} = \frac{4}{12}$

So $\frac{1}{3} = \frac{2}{6} = \frac{4}{12}$

But $\frac{1}{3}$ is the **simplest form**

1. Now find equivalent fractions for the following, using multiplication.

(a) $\dfrac{1^{\times 2}}{4^{\times 2}} = \boxed{\phantom{-}}$   (b) $\dfrac{1^{\times 3}}{4^{\times 3}} = \boxed{\phantom{-}}$   (c) $\dfrac{1^{\times 2}}{5^{\times 2}} = \boxed{\phantom{-}}$   (d) $\dfrac{1^{\times 2}}{6^{\times 2}} = \boxed{\phantom{-}}$   (e) $\dfrac{5^{\times 2}}{6^{\times 2}} = \boxed{\phantom{-}}$

(f) $\dfrac{3}{6} = \boxed{\phantom{-}}$   (g) $\dfrac{3}{4} = \boxed{\phantom{-}}$   (h) $\dfrac{1}{3} = \boxed{\phantom{-}}$   (i) $\dfrac{2}{3} = \boxed{\phantom{-}}$   (j) $\dfrac{2}{6} = \boxed{\phantom{-}}$

Dividing the number above the line and the number below the line of a fraction by the same number will bring the fraction to its simplest form.

$$\frac{4^{\div 2}}{8^{\div 2}} = \frac{2^{\div 2}}{4^{\div 2}}\ \frac{1}{2}\ \text{or}\ \frac{4^{\div 4}}{8^{\div 4}} = \frac{1}{2}$$

$$\frac{8^{\div 4}}{12^{\div 4}} = \frac{2}{3}$$

2. Use division to write these fractions in their simplest form.

(a) $\dfrac{6^{\div 2}}{10^{\div 2}} = \boxed{\phantom{-}}$   (b) $\dfrac{10^{\div 2}}{12^{\div 2}} = \boxed{\phantom{-}}$   (c) $\dfrac{6^{\div 6}}{12^{\div 6}} = \boxed{\phantom{-}}$   (d) $\dfrac{9^{\div 3}}{12^{\div 3}} = \boxed{\phantom{-}}$

(e) $\dfrac{2}{6} = \boxed{\phantom{-}}$   (f) $\dfrac{3}{6} = \boxed{\phantom{-}}$   (g) $\dfrac{6}{10} = \boxed{\phantom{-}}$   (h) $\dfrac{2}{4} = \boxed{\phantom{-}}$

(i) $\dfrac{3}{9} = \boxed{\phantom{-}}$   (j) $\dfrac{8}{10} = \boxed{\phantom{-}}$   (k) $\dfrac{6}{9} = \boxed{\phantom{-}}$   (l) $\dfrac{4}{6} = \boxed{\phantom{-}}$

3. Simplify the fractions in these mixed numbers using the division method.

(a) $2\frac{6}{10} = 2\boxed{\phantom{-}}$   (b) $4\frac{2}{8} = 4\boxed{\phantom{-}}$   (c) $1\frac{2}{6} = 1\boxed{\phantom{-}}$   (d) $2\frac{3}{9} = 2\boxed{\phantom{-}}$   (e) $3\frac{3}{12} = 3\boxed{\phantom{-}}$

# Little and large

Look at these two rubbish bins.
Would you say that they are equivalent?
No, I don't think so because one is much
bigger than the other. They certainly are
not equivalent.

What do you think the big bin is saying to
the little bin? To find out, all you have to do
is take the fractions and the letters that go with
them out of the bin and match them with their
equivalent fractions in the grid. The first one is done for you.

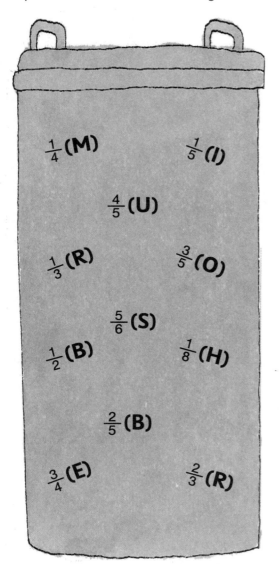

Fractions in the big bin:
$\frac{1}{4}$ (M)　$\frac{1}{5}$ (I)
$\frac{4}{5}$ (U)
$\frac{1}{3}$ (R)　$\frac{3}{5}$ (O)
$\frac{5}{6}$ (S)
$\frac{1}{2}$ (B)　$\frac{1}{8}$ (H)
$\frac{2}{5}$ (B)
$\frac{3}{4}$ (E)　$\frac{2}{3}$ (R)

| $\frac{2}{8}$ | $\frac{6}{10}$ | $\frac{4}{6}$ | $\frac{9}{12}$ |
|---|---|---|---|
| $\frac{1}{4}$ | | | |
| M | | | |

| $\frac{3}{9}$ | $\frac{8}{10}$ | $\frac{6}{12}$ | $\frac{4}{10}$ | $\frac{2}{10}$ | $\frac{10}{12}$ | $\frac{2}{16}$ |
|---|---|---|---|---|---|---|
| | | | | | | |
| | | | | | | |

## Chapter 8
### Decimals 1

**You need:**
– a calculator

### A Looking back

We use decimals when we are dealing with money.

 10c is $\frac{1}{10}$ of  (1 euro) and is written like this: €0.10.

1. (a) 20c = $\frac{\boxed{\phantom{0}}}{10}$ of  = €0._____   (b) 40c = $\frac{\boxed{\phantom{0}}}{10}$ of  = €_____._____

   (c) 80c = $\frac{\boxed{\phantom{0}}}{10}$ of  = €_____.   (d) 90c = $\frac{\boxed{\phantom{0}}}{10}$ of  = €_____.

 1c = $\frac{1}{100}$ of  and is written like this: €0.01.

2. (a) 2c = $\frac{\boxed{\phantom{0}}}{100}$ of  = €0._____   (b) 5c = $\frac{\boxed{\phantom{0}}}{100}$ of  = €_____.

   (c) 7c = $\frac{\boxed{\phantom{0}}}{100}$ of  = €_____.   (d) 9c = $\frac{\boxed{\phantom{0}}}{100}$ of  = €_____.

3.  = €1 + $\frac{5}{10}$ + $\frac{1}{100}$ = €1.51

4.  = €___ + $\frac{\boxed{\phantom{0}}}{10}$ + $\frac{\boxed{\phantom{0}}}{100}$ = €_____.

5. What is the value of the red digit in each sum of money?
   (a) €7.85 _____ (b) €10.96 _____ (c) €24.09 _____ (d) €125.84 _____ (e) €95.87 _____

6. Put these decimals in order starting with the smallest.

   (a) 3.78, 3.85, 3.26, 3.59    _____  _____  _____  _____

   (b) 1.69, 1.58, 1.67, 1.63    _____  _____  _____  _____

7. Write the missing decimals in these sequences.
   (a) 2.78, 2.79, _____, _____, 2.82, _____, _____
   (b) 5.52, _____, _____, 5.49, 5.48, _____, _____

8. (a) Find the total cost of this pair of jeans and
       the sweatshirt. _____

   (b) What is the difference in price between the
       jeans and the sweatshirt? _____

   (c) Check your answers using a calculator.

€39.50  €34.59

# Thousandths

**B   Moving on**

Decimals are often used when we deal with length, weight and capacity.

This runner is 179cm tall.                    179cm  = **1.79 metres**

She weighs 49kg 850g.                        49kg 850g = **49.85kg**

She is drinking from a 750ml bottle of water.    750ml  =  **0.75 litres**

1. (a)        1 kilogram    = 1000 grammes.

   (b)        100g    = (one tenth) $\frac{1}{10}$ kg        = 0.1 kg.

   (c)        10g     = (one hundredth) $\frac{1}{100}$ kg   = 0.01 kg.

   (d)        1g      = (one thousandth) $\frac{1}{1000}$ kg = 0.001 kg.

2. Check the weights marked on items of food at home and fill the grid, using two items of food in each case.

   < less than
   > more than

| < 100g | (a) | (b) |
|---|---|---|
| < 500g | (a) | (b) |
| > 1kg | (a) | (b) |

# Decimals in weight

1. (a) $100g = \boxed{\frac{1}{10}}$ kg = **0.1** kg

   (b) $200g = \boxed{\frac{2}{10}}$ kg = **0.2** kg

   (c) $400g = \boxed{\frac{\phantom{4}}{10}}$ kg = _____ kg

   (d) $900g = \boxed{\frac{\phantom{9}}{\phantom{9}}}$ kg = _____ kg

2. (a) $10g = \boxed{\frac{1}{100}}$ kg = **0.01** kg

   (b) $20g = \boxed{\frac{2}{100}}$ kg = **0.02** kg

   (c) $50g = \boxed{\frac{\phantom{5}}{100}}$ kg = 0.0____ kg

   (d) $80g = \boxed{\frac{\phantom{8}}{100}}$ kg = 0.0____ kg

3. (a) $1g = \boxed{\frac{1}{1000}}$ kg = **0.001** kg

   (c) $7g = \boxed{\frac{\phantom{7}}{\phantom{7}}}$ kg = 0._____ kg

   (b) $2g = \boxed{\frac{2}{1000}}$ kg = _____ kg

   (d) $8g = \boxed{\frac{\phantom{8}}{\phantom{8}}}$ kg = 0._____ kg

---

$1256g =$          $1000g + 200g + 50g + 6g$

                  $1kg + \frac{2}{10} + \frac{5}{100} + \frac{6}{1000} = 1 \underset{\text{units}}{.} \underset{\text{tenths}}{2} \underset{\text{hundredths}}{5} \underset{\text{thousandths}}{6}$ kg

---

4. (a) $1367g = \underline{\ 1\ }$ kg $+ \boxed{\frac{3}{10}} + \boxed{\frac{6}{100}} + \boxed{\frac{7}{1000}} = \underline{1.367}$ kg

   (b) $1483g = \underline{\ \ \ }$ kg $+ \boxed{\frac{\phantom{x}}{\phantom{x}}} + \boxed{\frac{\phantom{x}}{\phantom{x}}} + \boxed{\frac{\phantom{x}}{\phantom{x}}} = \underline{\ \ \ \ .\ \ \ \ }$ kg

   (c) $2345g = \underline{\ \ \ }$ kg $+ \boxed{\frac{\phantom{x}}{\phantom{x}}} + \boxed{\frac{\phantom{x}}{\phantom{x}}} + \boxed{\frac{\phantom{x}}{\phantom{x}}} = \underline{\ \ \ \ .\ \ \ \ }$ kg

5. (a) $3025g = \underline{\ 3\ }$ kg $+ \boxed{\frac{0}{10}} + \boxed{\frac{2}{100}} + \boxed{\frac{5}{1000}} = \underline{3.025}$ kg

   (b) $4063g = \underline{\ \ \ }$ kg $+ \boxed{\frac{\phantom{x}}{\phantom{x}}} + \boxed{\frac{\phantom{x}}{\phantom{x}}} + \boxed{\frac{\phantom{x}}{\phantom{x}}} = \underline{\ \ \ \ .\ \ \ \ }$ kg

   (c) $5072g = \underline{\ \ \ }$ kg $+ \boxed{\frac{\phantom{x}}{\phantom{x}}} + \boxed{\frac{\phantom{x}}{\phantom{x}}} + \boxed{\frac{\phantom{x}}{\phantom{x}}} = \underline{\ \ \ \ .\ \ \ \ }$ kg

6. (a) $2506g = \underline{\ 2\ }$ kg $+ \boxed{\frac{5}{10}} + \boxed{\frac{0}{100}} + \boxed{\frac{6}{1000}} = \underline{2.506}$ kg

   (b) $6309g = \underline{\ \ \ }$ kg $+ \boxed{\frac{\phantom{x}}{\phantom{x}}} + \boxed{\frac{\phantom{x}}{\phantom{x}}} + \boxed{\frac{\phantom{x}}{\phantom{x}}} = \underline{\ \ \ \ .\ \ \ \ }$ kg

   (c) $4203g = \underline{\ \ \ }$ kg $+ \boxed{\frac{\phantom{x}}{\phantom{x}}} + \boxed{\frac{\phantom{x}}{\phantom{x}}} + \boxed{\frac{\phantom{x}}{\phantom{x}}} = \underline{\ \ \ \ .\ \ \ \ }$ kg

7. (a) $3950g = \underline{\ 3\ }$ kg $+ \boxed{\frac{9}{10}} + \boxed{\frac{5}{100}} + \boxed{\frac{0}{1000}} = \underline{3.95}$ kg

   (b) $8420g = \underline{\ \ \ }$ kg $+ \boxed{\frac{\phantom{x}}{\phantom{x}}} + \boxed{\frac{\phantom{x}}{\phantom{x}}} + \boxed{\frac{\phantom{x}}{\phantom{x}}} = \underline{\ \ \ \ .\ \ \ \ }$ kg

# Decimals in length and capacity

Remember!    1 litre = 1000 ml.

(a) 1l 705ml = 1.705l          (b) 2l 650ml = 2.65l          (c) 6l 37ml = 6.037l

1.  Write these as litres using the decimal point.

(a) 1l 317ml = _____._____          (b) 3l 307ml = _____._____

(c) 3l 26ml = _____._____          (d) 5l 250ml = _____._____

Remember! 1km = 1000 metres.

2.  Write these as kilometres using the decimal point.

(a) 255m = _____._____          (b) 478m = _____._____          (c) 109m = _____

(d)  86m = _____._____          (e)   9m = _____._____          (f)   7m = _____

|  | units | | tenths | hundredths | thousandths |
| --- | --- | --- | --- | --- | --- |
| | 8 | . | 6 | 2 | 5 |
| | 8km | | 600m | 20m | 5m |

3.  Write the value of the red digits in metres.

(a) 1.365km = _____ m          (b) 2.306km = _____ m     (c) 4.739km = _____ m

(d) 1.618km = _____ m          (e) 6.023km = _____ m     (f) 8.906km = _____ m

4.  Put in the correct symbol, **<** , **>** or **=** between each pair.

(a) 6.255   6.522          (b) 10.025   10.502          (c) 2.716   2.617          (d) 3.007   3.07

(e) 9.25    9.250          (f)  4.081    4.018          (g) 8.103   8.310          (h) 5.102   5.12

(i) 16.9    16.09          (j) 27.61    26.610          (k) 7.0     0.7            (l) 100.1   100.01

5.  Write these digits 6, 0, 4, 9, 2 in the boxes below to make:

(a) the smallest number possible.

(b) the largest number possible.

# Addition of decimals

1l 850ml          955ml          65ml

How much liquid is contained in total in these bottles?

1 l 850ml =   1.850l
0 l 955ml =   0.955l
0 l  65ml =   0.065l
                2.870l

2 litres     870 ml

 Be sure to keep the decimal points in line.

1.  Liam cycled 1.525km to the shop          __ . __ __ __ km

    and a further 2.075km to school.      + __ . __ __ __ km
    _____

    How far did he cycle in all?              __ . __ __ __ km

2.  Work out the answers and then check using a calculator.

    (a)   12.068     (b)    6.475     (c)  12.170     (d)  26.040     (e)  18.374     (f)  24.596
           6.523             3.950           9.005          12.968           6.754           7.368
        +  5.900          + 0.016         + 3.989        +  6.000        + 19.389        +  0.747
    _____        _____        _____        _____        _____        _____

3.  Do these in your copy and check the answers using a calculator.
    (a) 6.4 + 19.07 + 22.175     (b) 12.765 + 8.6 + 2.176     (c) 14.3 + 29.67 + 8.134

    (d) 18.195 + 7.51 + 59     (e) 6.75 + 48 + 31.176     (f)  14 + 2.985 + 17.3

4.  Use your calculator to find out if these answers are correct.
    Put (✔) in the box if they are correct and (✘) if they are not.

    (a) 27 + 19.069 + 6.768 = 52.837     ☐     (b) 16.24 + 19.679 + 7 + 14.273 = 57.192     ☐

    (c) 156.076 + 43.924 + 60 = 260     ☐     (d) 79.84 + 6 + 124.59 + 17.3 = 277.73     ☐

47

# Further addition

1. Do these in your copy and use your calculator to check your answers.

   (a) 5.634 + 2.69 + 4.9 = _____    (b) 3.768 + 1.08 + 3.126 = _____

   (c) 6.24 + 17.629 + 87 = _____    (d) 25.63 + 8.175 + 0.75 = _____

   (e) 1.964 + 12.002 + 7.6 = _____    (f) 54.904 + 5.6 + 11.07 = _____

   (g) 29.1 + 15.75 + 8.207 = _____    (h) 28.95 + 32 + 14.185 = _____

2. Use your calculator to find the answers.

   (a) 4.126 + 5.874 = _____            (b) 96.375 + 3.625 = _____

   (c) 799.264 + 200.736 = _____        (d) 5438.001 + 4561.999 = _____

3. This man drives a delivery van for an electronics factory.

   (a) The three boxes he is delivering weigh 17.655kg, 25.5kg and 10.825kg.

   Find the total weight of the boxes. _____ kg

   (b) He keeps his petrol receipts to show to his supervisor at the factory. His last three receipts show the following amounts of petrol: 18.5 litres; 19.7 litres; 23.8 litres.

   How much petrol is that altogether? _____ l

   (c) He travelled 128.72km on Monday, 164.125km on Tuesday and 89.9km on Wednesday. How far did he travel in the three days? _____ km

   (d) Check your answers using a calculator.

# Subtraction of decimals

← 3.955km    5km →

Alison's house                                    Peter's house

How much closer to school is Alison's house than Peter's?

5km − 3.955km

$$\begin{array}{r} {}^4 5.{}^9\!\cancel{0}\,{}^9\!\cancel{0}\,{}^1\!0 \text{ km} \\ -\ 3.9\,5\,5 \text{ km} \\ \hline 1.0\,4\,5 \text{ km} \end{array}$$

Alison lives 1.045km or 1km 45m closer to the school than Peter.

**Example 2**

From 16.708 take 5.972:    16.708 − 5.972

$$\begin{array}{r} 1{}^5\!6.{}^{16}\!\cancel{7}\,{}^1\!0\,8 \\ 5.\,9\,7\,2 \\ \hline 10.\,7\,3\,6 \end{array}$$

 Remember to keep the decimal points in line!

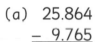

1. Check your answers using a calculator.

   (a)  25.864      (b)  23.572      (c)  41.620      (d)  38.254
       − 9.765          − 12.684         − 27.599         − 19.365

   _____          _____          _____          _____

2. Do these in your copy and check your answers using a calculator.

   (a) 32.650 − 17.762 _____   (b) 26.648 − 8.876 _____   (c) 11.654 − 6.587 _____

   (d) 24.060 − 18.754 _____   (e) 49.068 − 24.179 _____   (f) 36.001 − 9.895 _____

3. Use your calculator to find out if these answers are correct.
   Put a tick (✔) in the box if they are correct and (✖) if they are not.

   (a) 125 − 25.999 = 99.001 ☐         (b) 96.001 − 5.987 = 90.014 ☐

4. Make a good guess and then find the exact answer using a calculator.

   (a) 20 − 0.1      My guess: _____      Answer: _____

   (b) 100 − 0.001   My guess: _____      Answer: _____

# More subtraction

1. Do these in your copy and check your answers using a calculator.

(a) 5.627 – 3.738 = _____

(b) 8.109 – 5.679 = _____

(c) 3.098 – 1.75 = _____

(d) 9.185 – 4.99 = _____

(e) 12.6 – 5.758 = _____

(f) 26.01 – 19.825 = _____

(g) 90 – 39.829 = _____

(h) 100 – 75.999 = _____

2. Make a good guess and then find the exact answer using a calculator.

(a) 6.999 – 6.009    My Guess: _____    Answer: _____

(b) 26.825 – 26.025    My Guess: _____    Answer: _____

(c) 7.025 – 2.024    My Guess: _____    Answer: _____

(d) 19.999 – 19.99    My Guess: _____    Answer: _____

3.

**114.375kg** _____ _____ _____ _____

The sumo wrestler weighs 114.375kg! Use the information given below and a calculator to find out how much the other people in the picture weigh.
Write the correct weight under each picture.

(a) The boxer is 16.655kg lighter than the wrestler.

(b) The jockey is 41.95kg lighter than the boxer.

(c) The schoolgirl weighs 9.936kg less than the jockey.

(d) The schoolgirl is 30.875kg heavier than the infant.

50

# Michael's test

Here is a copy of a decimals test which Michael
did in fifth class. Can you check Michael's answers and put
✔ or ✗ in the boxes to show how well he did?
Use a calculator whenever possible.

Name:  Michael Good

Decimals Test        Fifth Class

1. 1,256kg = $1 + \frac{2}{10} + \frac{5}{100} + \frac{6}{1000}$ kg ☐

2. 1l 509ml = __1.509__ l ☐

3. 27m = __0.27__ km ☐

4. Fill in the missing decimal on this part of a number line ☐

9.77    9.78    9.79    9.8    9.81    9.82

5. 3.027, 3.028, 3.029, __3.3__ ☐

6. 9.997, 9.998, 9.999, __9.990__ ☐

Write the value of the red digits in metres.

7. 1.765km __700__ m ☐    8. 1.765km __5__ m ☐

9. 1.765km __100__ m ☐    10. 1.765km __60__ m ☐

Put in the correct symbol **<**, **>**, or **=**

11. 28.62 > 28.26 ☐    12. 4.052 < 4.502 ☐

13. 29.5 = 29.50 ☐    14. 16.51 < 16.511 ☐

15. 22.65 + 19.755 = __42.405__ ☐

16. 6.85 + 17 + 27.425 = __51.275__ ☐

17. 8.725 − 2.89 = __5.835__ ☐

18. 99 − 8.999 = __90.001__ ☐

19. What must be added to 25.875 to make 30? __5.125__ ☐

20. What must be subtracted from 36.196 to leave 36.006? __0.19__ ☐

**How did Michael do?**

**Correct answers:**

_____

**Incorrect answers:**

_____

51

1. Add these four numbers.

   734  +  8674  +  96  +  14 398 = _____

2. By how much is 960 bigger than 394? _____

3. Mr Maguire's car is 12 times cheaper than the bus he drives at work.
   The bus cost €234,000. Find the price of the car. €_____.

4. Find the cost of 16 litres of petrol at 91c a litre.  €_____._____.

5. Circle the even number: 25, 18, 39, 55.

6. Circle the odd number: 64, 72, 33, 16.

7. Colour in the square numbers on this part of the 100 square.

| 21 | 22 | 23 | 24 | 25 | 26 | 27 | 28 | 29 | 30 |
|----|----|----|----|----|----|----|----|----|----|
| 31 | 32 | 33 | 34 | 35 | 36 | 37 | 38 | 39 | 40 |
| 41 | 42 | 43 | 44 | 45 | 46 | 47 | 48 | 49 | 50 |
| 51 | 52 | 53 | 54 | 55 | 56 | 57 | 58 | 59 | 60 |

8. Colour in $\frac{2}{3}$ of this shape.

9. What fraction of this shape is coloured?
   Write the fraction in its simplest form.  $\boxed{—}$

10. Find $\frac{5}{8}$ of 96. _____

11.

    This is $\frac{3}{10}$ of Áine's money.
    How much money has she? €_____.

# Time to look back 2

12. Fill in the missing number     $\frac{2}{5} = \boxed{\frac{\phantom{0}}{10}}$

13. Put these numbers in order beginning with the largest:

| 2.18 | 2.81 | 8.21 | 8.12 | 6.956 | 6.596 |

_____  _____  _____  _____  _____  _____

14. Add these numbers: 3.56 + 18.6 + 34.795 = _____

15. From 16.254 take 9.867. _____

16. Circle the number between 80 and 89 that is both square and odd.

| 80 | 81 | 82 | 83 | 84 | 85 | 86 | 87 | 88 | 89 |

17. Dermot got €150 from his 3 aunties at Christmas.
He spent $\frac{3}{5}$ of it on computer games.
How much did he spend? _____

18. Marian lives 5km from the school. Her friend
Ruth is 1.25km nearer than that to the school.
How far from the school does Ruth live? _____

19. Last Friday only $\frac{3}{4}$ of the children in
St Malachy's were at school. If 60 were present,
how many children were absent? _____

20. Paul's Dad had 19.5 litres of petrol in his car. The car used 12.75 litres on a trip
to the seaside.
How many litres were still left in the tank? _____

How well did you do? Tick the box that shows your score.

| ☐ | ☐ | ☐ | ☐ |
| 18 – 20 | 15 – 17 | 10 – 14 | 0 – 9 |
| Excellent | Very good | Good | Keep up the good work |

# Chapter 10

## Length

**You need:**
- a ruler
- a metre stick
- a calculator
- a tape measure
- a trundle wheel

## A   Looking back

Carpenters and other workers need to be very accurate when measuring. See how accurate your answers to the following questions will be.

**1m = 100cm**          **1km = 1000m**

1.  Change to m and cm.

    (a) 265cm = _____m _____cm          (b) 305cm = _____m _____cm

2.  Change to km and m.

    (a) 1251m = _____km _____m          (b) 2375m = _____km _____m

3.  Write as metres in decimal form.

    (a) 325cm = _____._____m          (b) 680cm = _____._____m

4.  Write as km in decimal form.

    (a) 1249m = _____._____km          (b) 7075m = _____._____km

5.  Write as km and m.

    (a) 26.5km = _____km _____m          (b) 129.75km = _____km _____m

6.  (a)  | m | cm |
        |---|---|
        | 27 | 16 |
        | + 13 | 58 |

    (b)  | km | m |
        |---|---|
        | 16 | 240 |
        | + 13 | 865 |

    (c)  | m |
        |---|
        | 28.85 |
        | + 17.15 |

    (d)  | km |
        |---|
        | 36.75 |
        | + 15.50 |

7.  (a)  | m | cm |
        |---|---|
        | 26 | 90 |
        | − 12 | 59 |

    (b)  | km | m |
        |---|---|
        | 15 | 380 |
        | − 9 | 635 |

    (c)  | m |
        |---|
        | 16.85 |
        | − 8.60 |

    (d)  | km |
        |---|
        | 72.36 |
        | − 39.75 |

8.  (a) 16m 24cm
        × 4

    (b) 23km 460 m
        × 3

    (c) 7.45 m
        × 6

    (d) 18.35 km
        ×10

9.  (a) 5 ⟌ 37m 50cm          (b) 4 ⟌ 25km 324m          (c) 7 ⟌ 64.47m          (d) 6 ⟌ 127.68km

# The long and the short of it

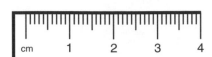

 We use millimetres to measure very short lengths. 1 centimetre = 10 millimetres
1cm = 10mm

| 1cm = 10mm | 1m = 100cm | 1km = 1000m |
|---|---|---|

This dust mite is less than one millimetre in length!

A hummingbird's beak can be up to 10cm in length – longer than its body!

A blue whale can grow to 33 metres in length!

A cheetah can reach speeds of 100km per hour!

1.  Write whether you would use mm, cm, m or km to measure the following:

    (a) the length of a corridor _____

    (b) the length of your arm _____

    (c) the thickness of your copy _____

    (d) the length of an ant _____

    (e) the width of your desk or table _____

    (f) your teacher's height _____

    (g) the distance between Cork and Dublin _____

    (h) the length of an eyelash _____

2.  Think of some examples yourself:

    I would use mm to measure _____

    I would use cm to measure _____

    I would use  m to measure _____

    I would use km to measure _____

3.  Ask your teacher and an adult at home about places or buildings which are approximately one kilometre from your school or home.

# Estimate and measure

Estimate the length of the following and then choose a ruler, a metre stick, a tape measure, or a trundle wheel to find the exact measurements.

|   | ESTIMATE | EXACT MEASUREMENT |
|---|---|---|
| 1 | | |
| 2 | | |
| 3 | | |
| 4 | | |
| 5 | | |
| 6 | | |
| 7 | | |
| 8 | | |
| 9 | | |
| 10 | | |
| 11 | | |
| 12 | | |
| 13 | | |
| 14 | | |
| 15 | | |
| 16 | | |
| 17 | | |
| 18 | | |
| 19 | | |
| 20 | | |

1. Length of the classroom.

2. The width of the nail on your little finger.

3. The distance from your desk to the window.

4. The width of a notebook.

5. The thickness of a coin.

6. The height of the classroom door.

7. The width of the classroom window.

8. The length of your pencil.

9. The length of your table.

10. The thickness of an eraser.

And now when you are out and about, find . . .

11. The length of a football pitch.

12. The width of a basketball court.

13. The length of a car.

14. The length of your longest stride.

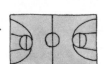

15. How far you can roll a football.

16. How far you can roll a €2 coin.

17. How far you can walk in 30 seconds.

18. How far you can run in 10 seconds.

19. The height of a postbox.

20. The height of a telephone kiosk.

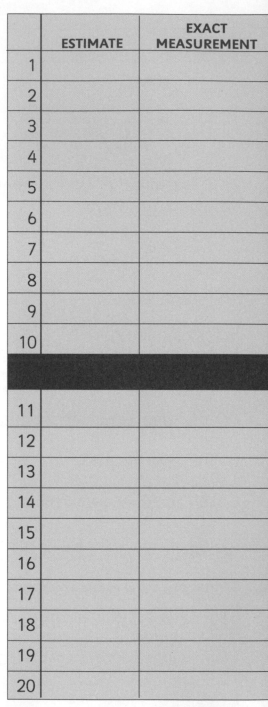

# How far?

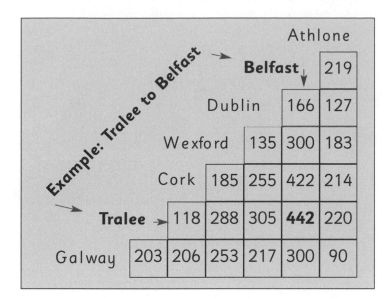

You will find grids like this one on road maps to help you work out distances in km between towns and cities. The example on this grid shows that Tralee is approximately 442km from Belfast.

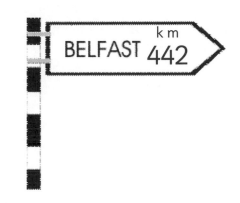

1. Find the distance between

   (a) Cork and Belfast _____

   (b) Wexford and Dublin _____

   (c) Dublin and Galway _____

   (d) Athlone and Galway _____

   (e) Tralee and Wexford _____

   (f) Dublin and Athlone _____

2. It is the same distance from Belfast to Galway as it is from Belfast to _____

3. Of the seven places listed beside the grid, Dublin is

   (a) nearest to _____

   (b) farthest from _____

4. James and John both live in Galway.
   (a) James and his family drove to Wexford this summer.
       How far was the round trip? _____

   (b) John and his Dad went to Belfast for a few days.
       How long was their round trip? _____

   (c) Find the difference in length between the two trips. _____

   (d) If John's Dad averaged 60km per hour on the journey to Belfast,
       how many hours did the drive take? _____

5. John's older brother works in Cork. He drove to Galway on Saturday and back to Cork on Sunday. How far did he drive on the round trip? _____ km

# Perimeter

The perimeter of a shape is the length around its sides.

These children have decided to put a low metal fence around this flowerbed. They used a trundle wheel and measured the length of the sides of the flowerbed to find out how many metres of fencing they needed. They found the **perimeter** of the flower bed.

Perimeter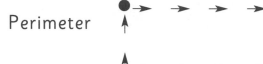

Estimate first and then find the perimeter of these irregular shapes by measuring the length of the sides.

(a)

Estimate: _____

Exact perimeter: _____

(b)

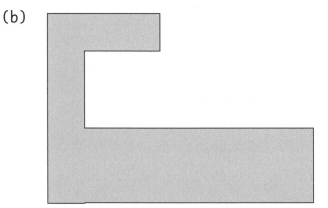

Estimate: _____

Exact perimeter: _____

(c)

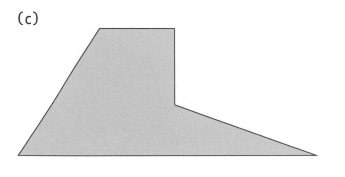

Estimate: _____

Exact perimeter: _____

(d)

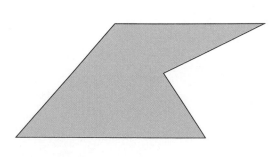

Estimate: _____

Exact perimeter: _____

# More perimeters

Name each shape. Estimate and then measure the perimeter of each shape.

(a)

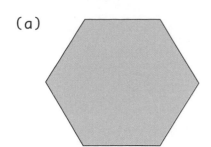

Shape: _____  Estimate: _____

Exact perimeter: _____

(b)

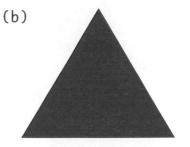

Shape: _____  Estimate: _____

Exact perimeter: _____

(c)

Shape: _____  Estimate: _____

Exact perimeter: _____

(d)

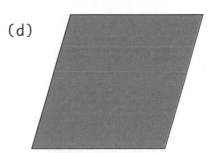

Shape: _____  Estimate: _____

Exact perimeter: _____

(e)

Shape: _____  Estimate: _____

Exact perimeter: _____

(f)

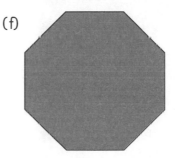

Shape: _____  Estimate: _____

Exact perimeter: _____

(g)

Shape: _____  Estimate: _____

Exact perimeter: _____

(h)

Shape: _____  Estimate: _____

Exact perimeter: _____

# Perimeter of rectangles and squares

Measure the perimeter of this rectangle.
Perimeter of this rectangle = _____
2 x Length + 2 x Width
= (2 x 6cm) + (2 x 4cm)
= 12cm + 8cm = 20cm
The perimeter of this rectangle is 20cm.

Perimeter of a rectangle = 2L + 2W.

L = Length
W = Width

1. Now find the perimeter of the following rectangles.
   (a) L = 10cm  W = 5cm    Perimeter: _____

   (b) L = 25cm  W = 12cm   Perimeter: _____

   (c) L = 36m   W = 21m    Perimeter: _____

2. How many metres of fencing would a farmer need for a field 50m
   in length and 40m in width with a gate 2m in width? _____

3.

   Measure the perimeter of this square. _____

   Perimeter of this square
   = 4 x Length of one side
   = 4 x 5cm = _____cm.

   Perimeter of a square = 4 x Length of one side.

4. Now find the perimeters of the following squares if one side measures

   (a) 7cm  Perimeter: _____      (b) 13cm   Perimeter: _____

   (c) 24m  Perimeter: _____      (d) 19cm   Perimeter: _____

   (e) 38m  Perimeter: _____      (f) 52.5cm Perimeter: _____

5. What length is the perimeter of

   (a) a maths copy? _____        (b) your desk or table? _____

   (c) a square centimetre? _____ (d) a square metre? _____

   (e) the black or whiteboard? _____  (f) your classroom? _____

# Problems for you to solve

Look at these pictures and then answer the questions below.

1. The football field is 180 metres long and 100 metres wide. A man puts a white line all the way around the outside.
   How long is that line? _____

2. How many metres of tape would be needed to mark the outside edge of the basketball court if it measures 16m in length and 9m in width? _____

3. (a) How many metres of the paper border are needed in the coffee shop if it measures 12m in length and 8m in width? _____
   (b) How many rolls of border are needed if each roll is 10m long? _____

4. The 25m swimming pool is 12.75m wide. How long is the grip rail in the pool? _____

5. The young trees outside the leisure centre are 75cm in height.
   They will be five times that height when they are fully grown.
   To what height will they grow? _____m _____cm

6. Check your answers using a calculator.

# Use your head

Try doing these in your head.

1. 6.3cm = _____ cm _____ mm

2. 26.9m = _____ m _____ cm

3. 2.125km = _____ km _____ m

4. 10cm = _____ mm

5. 1m = _____ mm

6. 1km = _____ cm

7. 2.5m + 1$\frac{1}{2}$m = _____

8. 3km 500m + 4.75km = _____

9. 12m 60cm – 6.5m = _____

10. 24.5m – 6$\frac{1}{4}$m = _____

11. 3.2cm x 6 = _____ cm _____ mm

12. 16km 500m x 3 = _____ km _____ m

13. 16m 20cm ÷ 4 = _____ m _____ cm

14. 15.4km ÷ 7 = _____ km _____ m

15. Put these lengths in order starting with the shortest: 2.65m, 2m 5cm, 2m, and 2$\frac{1}{10}$ m.

_____        _____        _____        _____

16. How many centimetres in 2.6m? _____ cm

17. How many metres in 3.125km? _____ m

18. Deirdre is 1.4m tall and her father is 42cm taller than Deirdre. How tall is Deirdre's father? _____

19. Deirdre's mother is 0.07m shorter than Deirdre's father. How tall is Deirdre's mother? _____

20. Deirdre's little sister Pauline is half Deirdre's height.
    (a) How much taller than Pauline is her father? _____
    (b) How much shorter than her mother is Pauline? _____

21. How much taller than Deirdre is her mother? _____

# Fun with height

Name: _____ _____ _____ _____

Height: _____ _____ _____ _____

1. Read these two sentences and write the correct name under each child in the picture.

   (a) Joan's friend Susan wears glasses.

   (b) Tom's brother Jack is wearing a navy sweatshirt.

2. Read the following three sentences and write each child's correct height under his or her name.

   (a) Susan is 127.5cm tall.

   (b) Jack is 5.3cm taller than Susan.

   (c) Joan is 3.6cm shorter than Susan.

   (d) If Tom was 3cm taller he would be 2cm taller than Susan.

3. Write out the children's names and heights starting with the shortest.

   Name: _____ _____ _____ _____

   Height: _____ _____ _____ _____

4. What is the difference in height between the tallest and the shortest child? _____

**You need:**
– a protractor
– a ruler
– a pencil
– a scissors
– cardboard or strong paper
– to revise angles

Do you still remember the 5 types of angles we learned about in Chapter 2 of this book?
Can you put the correct name under each angle?

(a)

_____

(b)

_____

(c)

_____

(d)  _____

(e)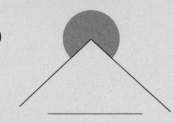

_____

## Measuring angles

If you want to find out how much water is in a bucket you use litres and millilitres.
To measure weight we can use kilogrammes and grammes.
To measure length we can use metres and centimetres.

But how do we measure angles? _____
Look at these two angles.

(a)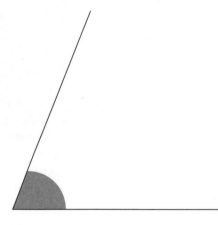

(b)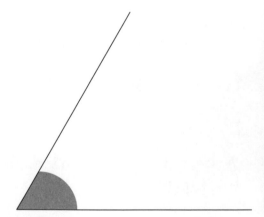

Which angle would you say is the bigger? _____

How do you know it is bigger? _____

# Angles

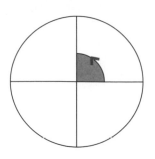

To be sure to get the correct answer to the last question on page 64 we need to measure both angles. Angles are measured in degrees. For example, there are 90 degrees in a right angle — that is $\frac{1}{4}$ of a full turn or rotation.

There are 180 degrees in a straight angle — that is $\frac{1}{2}$ of a full turn.

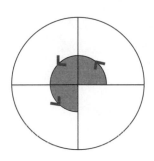

How many degrees in $\frac{3}{4}$ of a full rotation? _____
Yes, you're right. There are 270 degrees in this angle.

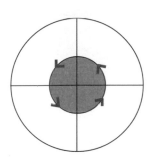

Now how many degrees in one full rotation? _____
Yes, you are right. There are 360 degrees in a full rotation.

The symbol for degrees is °. So 180 degrees is written as 180° and 90 degrees is written as 90°.

# Estimating angles

1. Look at these 9 angles.
   Which of them are

   (a) 90°? _____

   (b) greater than 90°? _____

   (c) less than 90°? _____

   (d) greater than 180°? _____

   Which do you think is

   (e) the smallest? _____

   (f) the largest? _____

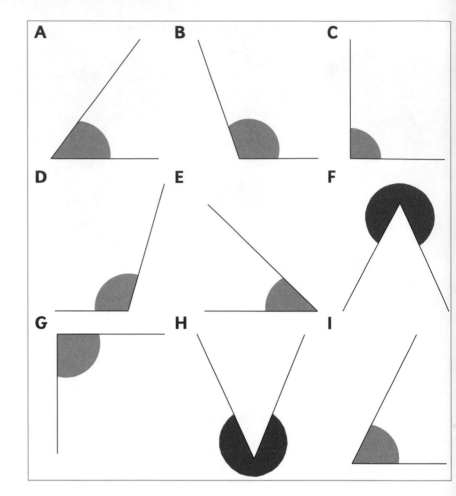

2. Look at these clock faces. Estimate the size of the angles between
   the hands in each case.

   (a)

   (b)

   (c)

   _____ _____ _____

   (d)

   (e)

   (f)

   _____ _____ _____

# Estimating angles

1. Estimate how many degrees in each of these angles.

(a)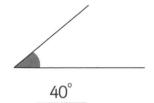

$\underline{40^{\circ}}$

(b)

_____

(c)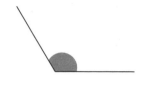

_____

(d)

(e)

(f)

(g)

_____

(h)

_____

(i)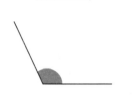

_____

_____

_____

_____

Remember!

A right angle ⌐ is 90°.

An acute angle ∠ is less than 90°.

An obtuse angle ∟ is greater than 90°.

A straight angle —○— is 180°.

A reflex angle ⌒ is greater than 180°.

2. Estimate the size of the angles in these shapes.

(a)

(b)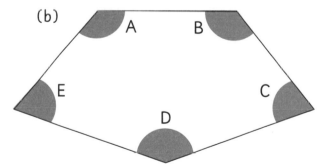

(i) Angle A = _____
(ii) Angle B = _____
(iii) Angle C = _____
(iv) Angle D = _____

(i) Angle A = _____
(ii) Angle B = _____
(iii) Angle C = _____
(iv) Angle D = _____
(v) Angle E = _____

# Measuring angles

To measure the exact size of an angle you need a **protractor.**

A protractor has:
- a centre point
- a base line
- two scales – an inner scale and an outer scale.

Each scale goes from 0° to 180°.

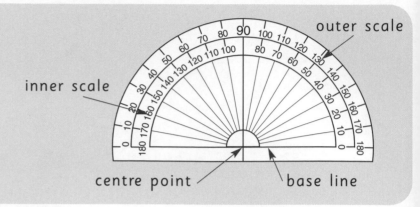

inner scale

outer scale

centre point          base line

This is how you measure the size of an angle:

- Make sure that the **base line** is along **one line** of the angle.

- Also ensure that the **centre point** is **directly** on the **point** of the angle.

(a) What size is this angle?

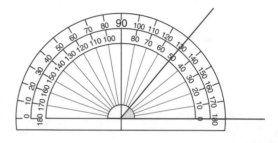

- The base line is on the line of the angle.

- The centre point is on the point of the angle.

- The angle is 50° (inner scale).

(b) What size is this angle?

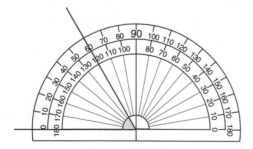

- The base line is on the line of the angle.

- The centre point is on the point of the angle.

- The angle is 60° (outer scale).

(c) What size is this angle?

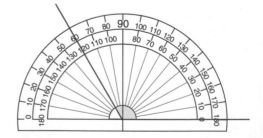

- The base line is on the line of the angle.

- The centre point is on the point of the angle.

- The angle is 120° (inner scale).

# Estimating and measuring angles

Look at these angles. Estimate the size of each angle first and then measure them with your protractor. Then find the difference between the two answers.

(a)

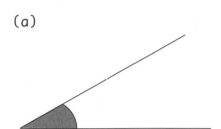

My Estimate: _____

Exact size: _____

Difference: _____

(b)

My Estimate: _____

Exact size: _____

Difference: _____

(c)

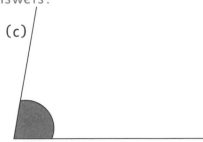

My Estimate: _____

Exact size: _____

Difference: _____

(d)

My Estimate: _____

Exact size: _____

Difference: _____

(e)

My Estimate: _____

Exact size: _____

Difference: _____

(f)

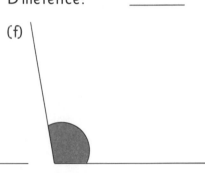

My Estimate: _____

Exact size: _____

Difference: _____

(g)

My Estimate: _____

Exact size: _____

Difference: _____

(h)

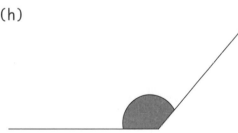

My Estimate: _____

Exact size: _____

Difference: _____

(i)

My Estimate: _____

Exact size: _____

Difference: _____

Compare your answers with those of a friend.

• Now go back to page 64. Measure the two angles at the end of the page.
  Are they the same size?  Yes ☐  No ☐

# Drawing an angle

**Example:** Draw an angle of 30°

(a)               (b)               (c)

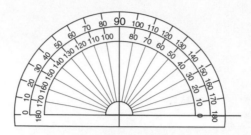

Draw a line about 4cm long.

Place the protractor on the line making sure that the base line is along this line and the centre point is at the beginning of the line.

Find 30° on the inner scale and put a mark with your pencil at the outside of your protractor.

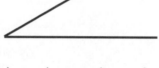

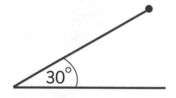

Now lift your protractor.

Join the mark to the beginning of the line.

The angle you have drawn is 30°.

1.  Use the inner scale to draw angles of
    (a) 30°               (b) 50°             (c) 100°

_____         _____         _____

2.  Use the outer scale to draw angles of
    (a) 15°               (b) 65°             (c) 140°

_____         _____         _____

3.  Draw these angles in your copy using a pencil, a ruler and a protractor.
    (a) 60°      (b) 45°      (c) 75°      (d) 40°
    (e) 120°    (f) 150°    (g) 110°    (h) 170°

# The angles in a triangle

1. Look at these 3 angles. First estimate how many
   degrees in each angle.
   Then, with your protractor, find the exact size of each angle.

The symbol for
an angle is ∠

(a)
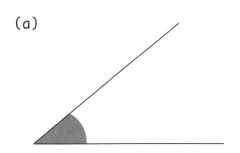

My estimate: _____

Exact size: _____

(b)

My estimate: _____

Exact size: _____

(c)
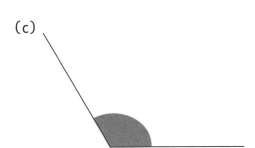

My estimate: _____

Exact size: _____

2. Now measure another 3 angles, but these 3 angles are
   in a triangle. Then find the sum of the 3 angles.

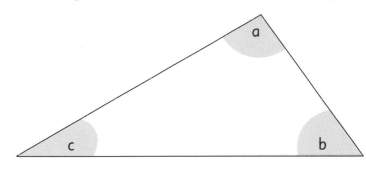

Measure of ∠ a = _____

Measure of ∠ b = _____

Measure of ∠ c = _____

Sum of the 3 angles = _____

3. Now find the sum of the 3 angles in these triangles.

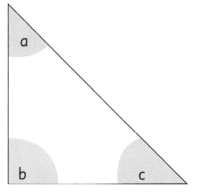

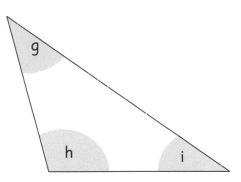

Sum of the 3 angles = _____    Sum of the 3 angles = _____    Sum of the 3 angles = _____

4. Look at the answers you got for the sum of the 3 angles in a triangle in
   Questions 2 and 3. Have you noticed anything about the answers?
   Compare them with the answers that the other children got.

# Angles in a triangle

1. For this question you will need: a piece of cardboard or strong paper; a scissors and a pencil.

    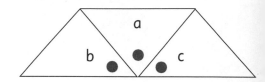

    (a) Draw a triangle on the piece of paper or cardboard.

    (b) Mark the angles with a, b and c.

    (c) Then cut out the angles.

    (d) Place the 3 angles side by side.

    (e) When the 3 angles are placed side by side, what kind of angle do they form?

    A <u>st – – – – – –</u> angle.

    (f) How many degrees in this kind of angle? _____

    (g) Fill in the missing words:

    | The _____ of the _____ angles in a triangle is _____. |

2. Find the size of the missing angle in each triangle.

    (a)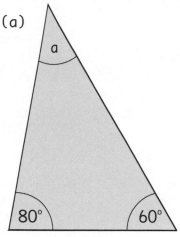

    (b)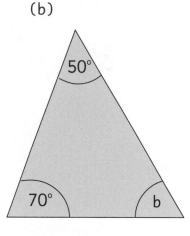

    (c)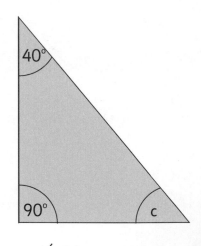

    ∠ (a) = _____        ∠ (b) = _____        ∠ (c) = _____

3. Fill in the size of ∠ (c) for each triangle.

    (a) Triangle 1:  ∠ (a) = 90°    ∠ (b) = 45°    ∠ (c) = _____

    (b) Triangle 2:  ∠ (a) = 65°    ∠ (b) = 55°    ∠ (c) = _____

    (c) Triangle 3:  ∠ (a) = 20°    ∠ (b) = 75°    ∠ (c) = _____

# Triangles again

1. Find the size of the missing angles

(a)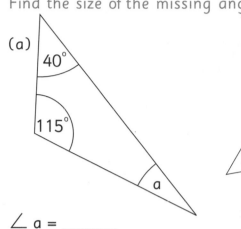

∠ a = _____

(b)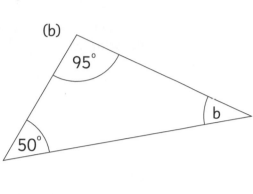

∠ b = _____

(c)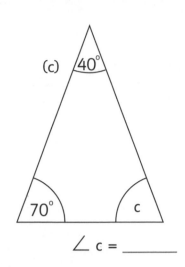

∠ c = _____

## Triangles Galore!

2. Do you like this drawing of a cat?

What shape is used to draw the cat?

How many triangles can you count? _____

(Choose one of the following numbers: 11, 8, 13)

- When you have counted all the triangles you can
  (a) colour the cat and   (b) give him/her a name.
- You know that the angles in a triangle add up to 180°.
  You can use a calculator to find out
  how many degrees are in all the triangles of this cat drawing. _____

Name of cat: _____

3. Draw any animal of your choice using triangles.

# Chapter 12

## 2-D Shapes

**You need :**
- a ruler
- a protractor
- a compass
- a mug or circular lid
- a scissors
- cm squared paper
- 2-D shapes
- to explain 'oblique'

A 2-D shape has two dimensions, height and width.

1. Unscramble the letters and then name the shapes.

_____    _____    _____    _____    _____    _____

csmirleice    geltinra     lavo      qaruse     rtgleecan    licrce

2.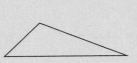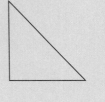

_____    _____    _____    _____

Read the descriptions and then name each triangle correctly.

Scalene: no equal sides             Equilateral: 3 equal sides
Right-angled: one angle is a right-angle (90°)    Isosceles: 2 equal sides

3.    A•        B •             A •        •B

    D•     •C

                             D•        •C

_____

(a) Use a ruler and pencil to join the dots to make two four-sided shapes.

(b) Read the descriptions and name the shapes correctly.   _____
Parallelogram: opposite sides are equal and parallel.
Rhombus: 4 equal sides and opposite sides are parallel.

4. 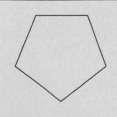 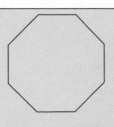 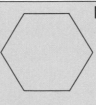    Name these regular shapes correctly
                                        octagon

                                        hexagon

                                        pentagon

_____    _____    _____

# Angles in quadrilaterals

A quadrilateral is a four-sided figure.

1. Name four quadrilaterals already mentioned in this chapter.

_____  _____  _____  _____

2. Measure the length of the sides and the size of the angles in these quadrilaterals and write the information below.

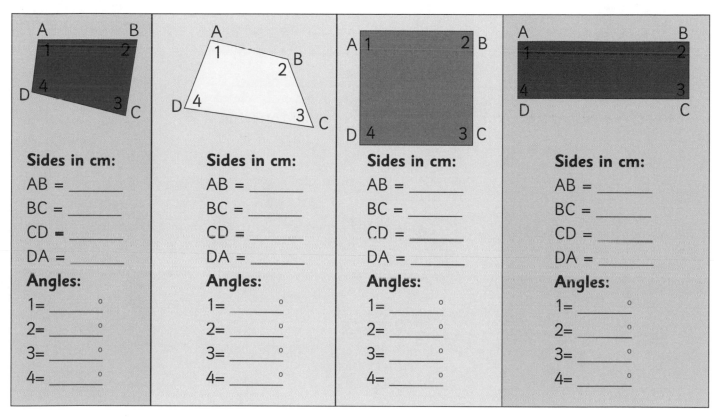

| Sides in cm: | Sides in cm: | Sides in cm: | Sides in cm: |
|---|---|---|---|
| AB = _____ | AB = _____ | AB = _____ | AB = _____ |
| BC = _____ | BC = _____ | BC = _____ | BC = _____ |
| CD = _____ | CD = _____ | CD = _____ | CD = _____ |
| DA = _____ | DA = _____ | DA = _____ | DA = _____ |
| **Angles:** | **Angles:** | **Angles:** | **Angles:** |
| 1= _____ ° | 1= _____ ° | 1= _____ ° | 1= _____ ° |
| 2= _____ ° | 2= _____ ° | 2= _____ ° | 2= _____ ° |
| 3= _____ ° | 3= _____ ° | 3= _____ ° | 3= _____ ° |
| 4= _____ ° | 4= _____ ° | 4= _____ ° | 4= _____ ° |

3. How many of the quadrilaterals in Question 2 have
   (a) 4 equal sides? _____
   (b) 4 sides of different lengths? _____
   (c) opposite sides which are equal in length? _____
   (d) 1 pair of parallel lines? _____
   (e) 2 pairs of parallel lines? _____
   (f) 4 equal angles? _____
   (g) 4 angles of different sizes? _____
   (h) 4 right angles? _____
   (i) opposite angles which are equal? _____
   (j) one or more angles greater than 90°? _____
   (k) lines that are perpendicular? _____

# More quadrilaterals

1.

This shape is called a trapezium. A trapezium has one pair of parallel lines.

Line _____ is parallel to line _____.

2. Now draw three trapeziums in your copy.

3. True or false?
   (a) All quadrilaterals have four sides and four angles. _____
   (b) A trapezium is a quadrilateral. _____

4. Name these shapes.

_____    _____         _____              _____

5. Fill in this grid by putting a tick (✓) or (✗) in each of these boxes.

You need to use a ruler and a protractor.

| | | Square | Rectangle | Parallelogram | Rhombus | Trapezium |
|---|---|---|---|---|---|---|
| (a) | Has four angles of equal size | | | | | |
| (b) | Has four sides of equal length | | | | | |
| (c) | Has opposite sides of equal length | | | | | |
| (d) | Has oblique lines | | | | | |
| (e) | Has lines that are perpendicular | | | | | |
| (f) | Opposite angles are equal | | | | | |
| (g) | Has right angles | | | | | |
| (h) | Number of pairs of parallel lines | | | | | |

6. True or false? All quadrilaterals

|  | True | False |
|---|---|---|
| (a) have at least one right angle | ☐ | ☐ |
| (b) have at least one obtuse angle | ☐ | ☐ |
| (c) have 2 pairs of parallel lines | ☐ | ☐ |
| (d) have 4 sides which are equal in length | ☐ | ☐ |
| (e) have 4 right angles | ☐ | ☐ |
| (f) have 4 sides and 4 angles | ☐ | ☐ |

# Triangles

**1.**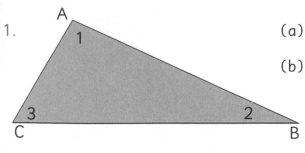

(a) A triangle has _____ sides and _____ angles.

(b) Find the sum of the angles in this triangle.

$\angle$ 1 = _____ °     $\angle$ 2 = _____ °     $\angle$ 3 = _____ °

Total = _____ °

**2.** Draw three triangles in your copy and

(a) find the sum of the angles in each triangle   (b) compare your angles with those of a friend.

**3.** Write the correct name under each triangle:
scalene, right-angled, isosceles or equilateral.

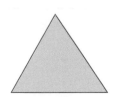         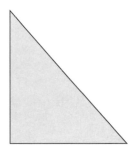

_____     _____     _____     _____

**4.** Fill in this grid about triangles by writing **Y** for Yes and **N** for No.

You will need to use a ruler and a protractor.

|     |                                  | Equilateral | Scalene | Isosceles | Right-angled |
|-----|----------------------------------|-------------|---------|-----------|--------------|
| (a) | Has 3 angles of equal size       |             |         |           |              |
| (b) | Has 2 angles of equal size       |             |         |           |              |
| (c) | Has 3 angles of different sizes  |             |         |           |              |
| (d) | Has 3 sides of equal length      |             |         |           |              |
| (e) | Has 2 sides of equal length      |             |         |           |              |
| (f) | Has 3 sides of different lengths |             |         |           |              |
| (g) | Has oblique lines                |             |         |           |              |
| (h) | Has lines that are perpendicular |             |         |           |              |
| (i) | Has parallel lines               |             |         |           |              |

# Time for a tangram!

This is a Chinese tangram. It is a square divided into seven separate pieces. The pieces can be used to construct 2-D shapes or pictures of animals or people, etc. – if you use your imagination!

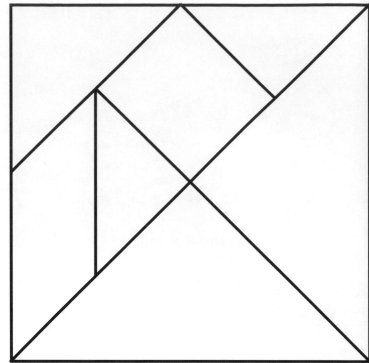

1.  List the 3 shapes used in the tangram.

    _____

    _____

    _____

2.  Circle the correct word:
    The triangles in the tangram are
    **equilateral, scalene**, **isosceles** or **right-angled.**

3.  (a) Trace the tangram and cut it into the seven separate shapes.

    (b) Can you make a cat like this using all seven tangram shapes?

4.  (a) Using 2 pieces, make a square.

    (b) Using 3 pieces, make a trapezium.

    (c) Using 4 pieces, make a rectangle.

    (d) Using 5 pieces, make a triangle.

5.  It is possible to make a rectangle, a triangle, a trapezium and a parallelogram using all seven pieces each time. Have a go!

# Circles

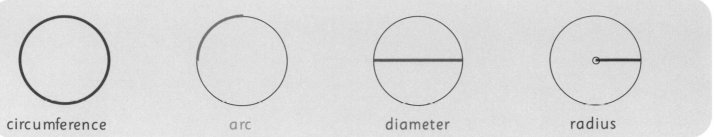

circumference      arc      diameter      radius

1. (a) Use a mug or the lid of a jar to draw four circles in your copy.

   (b) Use four different colours to draw and name the four parts of the circle as shown above.

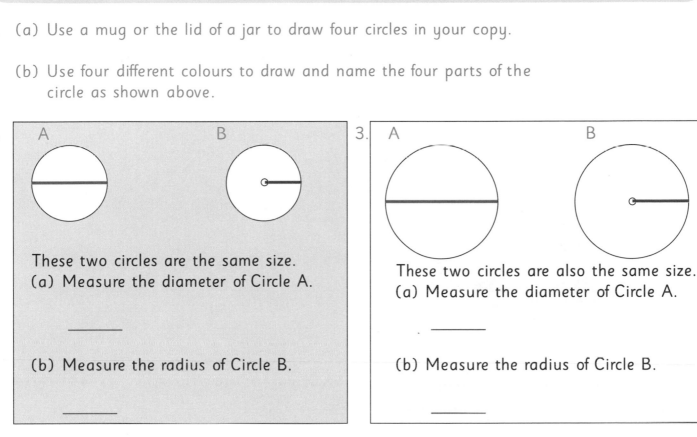

2.

A             B

These two circles are the same size.
(a) Measure the diameter of Circle A.

_____

(b) Measure the radius of Circle B.

_____

3.

A             B

These two circles are also the same size.
(a) Measure the diameter of Circle A.

. _____

(b) Measure the radius of Circle B.

_____

4. Fill the blanks in these sentences.

   (a) The diameter of a circle is _____ the length of the radius.

   (b) The radius of a circle is _____ the length of the diameter.

5. Find the radius of each circle if the diameter measures

   (a) 4cm _____    (b) 6cm _____    (c) 10cm _____    (d) 13cm _____    (e) 7cm _____

6. Find the diameter of each circle if the radius measures

   (a) 6cm _____    (b) 8cm _____    (c) 3.5cm _____    (d) 5.25cm _____    (e) 4.75cm _____

# Area of circles

1. With your compass and pencil draw a circle with a radius of 3 cm.

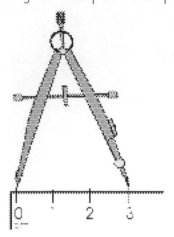

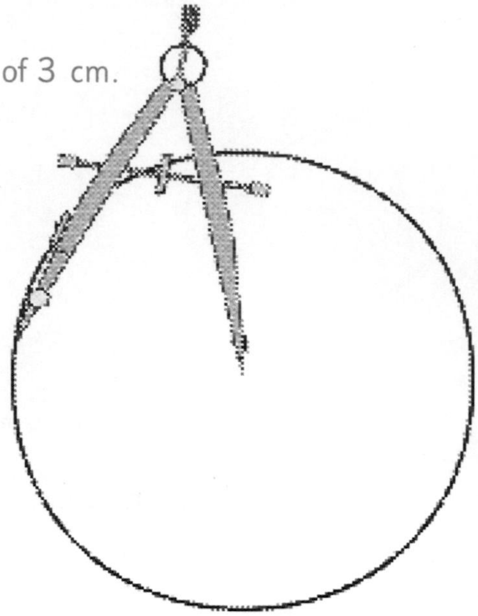

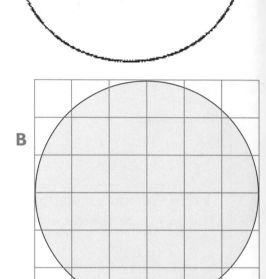

    (a) The radius of this circle is _____ cm.

    (b) The diameter of this circle is _____ cm.

2.

**A**

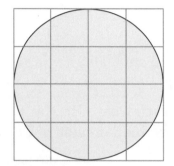

**B**

Count the square centimetres to
find the approximate area of these circles.
Count half a square or more as 1 sq. cm.
Less than half a square centimetre is not counted.

(a) Approximate area of Circle A = _____ cm². Circle B = _____ cm².

(b) Diameter of Circle A = _____ cm. Circle B = _____ cm.

(c) Radius of Circle A = _____ cm. Circle B = _____ cm.

3. On squared centimetre paper draw a circle with a radius of
    (a) 2cm    (b) 3cm    (c) 5cm    (d) 6cm    (e) 7cm

    Count the squares to find the approximate area of each circle.

    (a) _____    (b) _____    (c) _____    (d) _____    (e) _____

4. On squared centimetre paper draw circles with diameters of
    (a) 5cm    (b) 7cm    (c) 9cm    (d) 11cm    (e) 13cm

    Find the approximate area of the circles by counting the cm².

    (a) _____    (b) _____    (c) _____    (d) _____    (e) _____

# Lines of symmetry in 2-D shapes

1.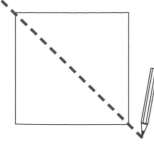

   (a) Draw in the missing lines of symmetry on this square.

   (b) A square has _____ lines of symmetry.

2. Now in your copy draw a rectangle, a circle, a semi-circle and a right-angled triangle and draw in the lines of symmetry in each shape.

3. Draw the lines of symmetry in these shapes.

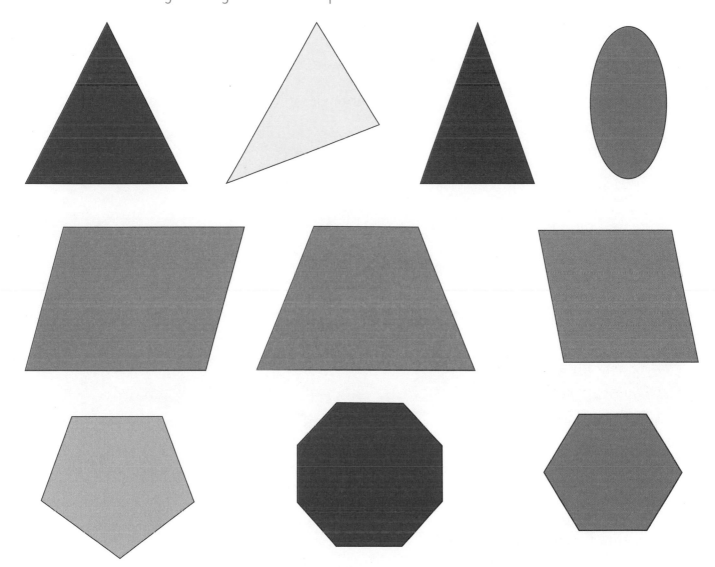

4. In your copy, list the names of the fifteen shapes you have worked on in Questions 1 to 3 on this page. Beside each one write the number of lines of symmetry you found.

   Compare and discuss your results with a friend.

# Tessellation

1. 2-D shapes tessellate if they fit together to cover a surface, without leaving gaps.

   (a)  Do squares tessellate? _____

   (b)  Do circles tessellate? _____

2. Do you think these shapes tessellate? Write **Yes** or **No** beside each one.

   (a) Rectangle _____   (b) Semi-circle _____   (c) Parallelogram _____

   (d) Trapezium _____   (e) Rhombus _____   (f) Pentagon _____

   (g) Octagon _____   (h) Hexagon _____   (i) Right-angled triangle _____

   (j) Scalene triangle _____   (k) Isosceles triangle _____   (l) Equilateral triangle _____

3. Using a set of 2-D shapes,

   (a) find out if the shapes listed in Question 2 tessellate.

   (b) check the answers you wrote in Question 2.

   (c) In your copy make a list of the 2-D shapes that you know do not tessellate.

4. Combinations of some 2-D shapes tessellate.

   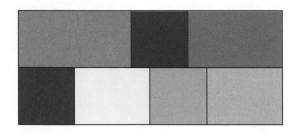
   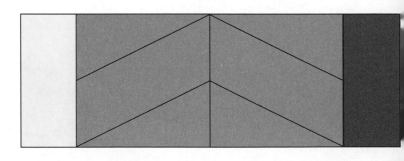

   (a) Name the 2 shapes used in this tessellation.

   _____ _____

   (b) What are the three shapes used in this tessellation?

   _____ _____ _____

5. Experiment with a set of 2-D shapes and in your copy make a list of pairs of 2-D shapes that tessellate.
   In your copy use combinations of 2-D shapes to draw your own tessellations.

# Robbie

1. Here is the captain of the Two-Dimensional Demons ready to play the final of the inter-planetary premiership league against the Galactic Greats!
   Look carefully and then write how many times each shape appears in the picture.

   (a) Square _____

   (b) Rectangle _____

   (c) Circle _____

   (d) Semi-circle _____

   (e) Oval _____

   (f) Equilateral triangle _____

   (g) Scalene triangle _____

   (h) Parallelogram _____

   (i) Rhombus _____

   (j) Pentagon _____

   (k) Hexagon _____

   (l) Octagon _____

   (m) Trapezium _____

   (n) Isosceles triangle _____

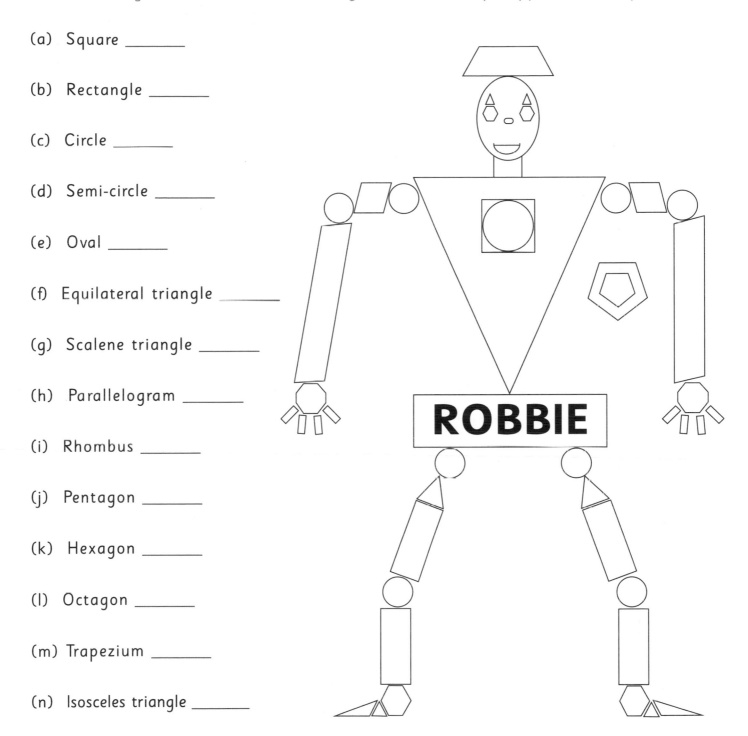

2. Now colour Robbie. In your copy, see if you can draw the captain of the Galactic Greats using each of the thirteen 2-D shapes at least once.

83

1. If you count up in 5's you get 5, 10, 15, 20, etc.
   The first four multiples of 5 are 5, 10, 15 and 20.

   (a) What is the next multiple of 5? _____

   (b) Write the next four multiples of 5 after 25: _____, _____, _____, _____.

2. The first 4 multiples of 3 are 3, 6, 9 and 12.

   (a) Write the next 4 multiples of 3. _____, _____, _____, _____

   (b) Write the 9th multiple of 3. _____    (c) Write the 11th multiple of 3. _____

   (d) What is the 12th multiple of 3? _____ (e) Write the 20th multiple of 3. _____

   (f) What is the lowest multiple of 3? _____

   (g) What is the highest multiple of 3? **(Be careful!)** _____

   (h) Put these multiples of 3 in order beginning with the lowest:
   33,     15,     18,     36,     24,     12,     3,     21,     9,     27,     6,     30

   ____  ____  ____  ____  ____  ____  ____  ____  ____  ____  ____  ____

3. (a) 4, 8, 12, 16, 20 are the multiples of which number? _____

   (b) Put these multiples in order beginning with the lowest:

   18,     30,     12,     48,     60,     42,     54,     6,     24,     36.

   ____  ____  ____  ____  ____  ____  ____  ____  ____  ____

   (c) Of what number are these the multiples? _____

   (d) Write the first 8 multiples of 2. ____ ____ ____ ____ ____ ____ ____ ____

   (e) Write the first 5 multiples of 10. ____ ____ ____ ____ ____

   (f) The number 10 is a c __ __ __ __ __ multiple as it appears in both lists.

# Factors

Look at this picture.
What is sold in this shop?
Yes, this shop sells parts for cars.
Another name for 'parts' is 'factors'.
Just as cars are made up of parts,
so also are numbers.

For example:      $8 = 4 \times 2$

and $8 = 8 \times 1$

The factors of 8 are 1, 2, 4 and 8.

Factors are also known as divisors.
When the number 8 is divided by 1, 2, 4 or 8 there is no remainder.

Why is 3 not a factor (divisor) of 8?
Because when 8 is divided by 3 there is a remainder of _____

$$3\overline{)8} \\ 2 \ r \ \rule{2cm}{0.4pt}$$

## $4 \quad \times \quad ? \quad = \quad 28$

Find the missing factor.

(a) $2 \times \text{\_\_\_\_} = 8$      (b) $3 \times \text{\_\_\_\_} = 6$      (c) $4 \times \text{\_\_\_\_} = 12$      (d) $10 \times \text{\_\_\_\_} = 10$

(e) $5 \times \text{\_\_\_\_} = 30$      (f) $\text{\_\_\_\_} \times 2 = 12$      (g) $\text{\_\_\_\_} \times 6 = 42$      (h) $\text{\_\_\_\_} \times 5 = 10$

(i) $4 \times \text{\_\_\_\_} = 20$      (j) $\text{\_\_\_\_} \times 8 = 24$      (k) $\text{\_\_\_\_} \times 7 = 35$      (l) $\text{\_\_\_\_} \times 4 = 32$

(m) $5 \times \text{\_\_\_\_} = 40$      (n) $9 \times \text{\_\_\_\_} = 81$      (o) $8 \times \text{\_\_\_\_} = 56$      (p) $9 \times \text{\_\_\_\_} = 18$

(q) $6 \times \text{\_\_\_\_} = 48$      (r) $\text{\_\_\_\_} \times 7 = 21$      (s) $5 \times \text{\_\_\_\_} = 45$      (t) $\text{\_\_\_\_} \times 6 = 54$

(u) $\text{\_\_\_\_} \times 9 = 36$      (v) $6 \times \text{\_\_\_\_} = 24$      (w) $4 \times \text{\_\_\_\_} = 28$      (x) $\text{\_\_\_\_} \times 7 = 63$

# Further factors

**Example**
List the factors of 6. Draw dot pictures to show these factors.

6 = 2 x 3

6 = 6 x 1

The factors of 6 are (1, 2, 3, 6).    The short way to write this is F6 = (1, 2, 3, 6)

1.  In your copy list the factors of the following numbers and
    draw dot pictures to show these factors.

    (a)  10          (b)  12          (c)  15          (d)  14          (e)  20

2.  In your copy list the factors of these numbers without using dot pictures.
    The first one is done for you.

    (a) 16 **F16 = (1, 2, 4, 8, 16)**    (b) 18      (c) 20    (d) 24    (e) 22
    (f)  25          (g) 28          (h) 30      (i) 32    (j) 36    (k) 40

3.

|     |     | TRUE | FALSE |
| --- | --- | :---: | :---: |
| (a) | 2 is a factor of 20 | ☐ | ☐ |
| (b) | 8 is a factor of 16 | ☐ | ☐ |
| (c) | 3 is a factor of 19 | ☐ | ☐ |
| (d) | 4 is a factor of 21 | ☐ | ☐ |
| (e) | 5 is a factor of 35 | ☐ | ☐ |
| (f) | 7 is a factor of 32 | ☐ | ☐ |
| (g) | 16 has only 4 factors | ☐ | ☐ |
| (h) | 22 has only 3 factors | ☐ | ☐ |
| (i) | 20 has only 5 factors | ☐ | ☐ |
| (j) | 40 has 8 factors | ☐ | ☐ |
| (k) | The highest factor of 50 is 25 | ☐ | ☐ |
| (l) | The lowest factor of 42 is 2 | ☐ | ☐ |

4.  Fill in the missing factors.

    (a)  F21 = (1, ____ 7, ____)        (b)    F27 = (____, ____, ____, 27)

    (c)  F35 = (1, ____, ____, ____)      (d)    F42 = (1, ____, 3, ____, ____, 14, ____, ____)

5.  What is the number:
    This number is greater than 13, less than 19 and has only two factors.

    The number is _____

# Prime and composite numbers

Write the factors of 7. F7 = ( _____ , _____ ).

What did you notice? Yes, 7 has only 2 factors, 1 and 7 itself.

Any number that has 2 and only 2 factors is called a **prime number.**

· The first prime number is 2 because F2 = (1, 2).

· 1 is not a prime number because it only has one factor F1 = (1).

A number that has more than 2 factors is called a **composite number.**

1.  Look at these numbers. List their factors and then write whether they are prime or composite.

   (a)  9 F9 = (1, 3, 9) composite _____        (b)  11 _____

   (c)  12 _____             (d)  15 _____

   (e)  13 _____             (f)  7 _____

   (g)  14 _____             (h)  19 _____

   (i)  18 _____             (j)  20 _____

   (k) 21 _____              (l)  22 _____

2.  (a) List all the prime numbers between 1 and 20.

   _____, _____, _____, _____, _____, _____, _____, _____.

   (b) List all the composite numbers between 1 and 20.

   _____, _____, _____, _____, _____, _____, _____, _____, _____, _____

3.  (a) Find the three composite numbers that are greater than 10 but
       less than 20, that have 5 or more factors each.

   _____, _____, _____

   (b) Write the factors here:

   F____ = ( _____ )  F____ = ( _____ )  F____ = ( _____ )

# What's a mathematician?

A mathematician is a person who is very interested in numbers. Are you a mathematician?

Long, long ago there lived a man in Greece who was very good at mathematics. His name was Eratosthenes. Just like you, he was very interested in prime numbers. He used the 100 square to separate the prime numbers from the composite numbers up as far as 100. Follow his instructions below and you will find all the prime numbers between 1 and 100. Use a pencil.

| 1 | 2 | 3 | 4 | 5 | 6 | 7 | 8 | 9 | 10 |
|---|---|---|---|---|---|---|---|---|---|
| 11 | 12 | 13 | 14 | 15 | 16 | 17 | 18 | 19 | 20 |
| 21 | 22 | 23 | 24 | 25 | 26 | 27 | 28 | 29 | 30 |
| 31 | 32 | 33 | 34 | 35 | 36 | 37 | 38 | 39 | 40 |
| 41 | 42 | 43 | 44 | 45 | 46 | 47 | 48 | 49 | 50 |
| 51 | 52 | 53 | 54 | 55 | 56 | 57 | 58 | 59 | 60 |
| 61 | 62 | 63 | 64 | 65 | 66 | 67 | 68 | 69 | 70 |
| 71 | 72 | 73 | 74 | 75 | 76 | 77 | 78 | 79 | 80 |
| 81 | 82 | 83 | 84 | 85 | 86 | 87 | 88 | 89 | 90 |
| 91 | 92 | 93 | 94 | 95 | 96 | 97 | 98 | 99 | 100 |

- Cross out 1.

- Circle the number 2 but cross out all the multiples of 2.

- Circle 3 but cross out all the multiples of 3.

- Circle 5 but cross out all the multiples of 5.

- Now circle 7 and cross out all the multiples of 7.

- Now circle all the other numbers that have not been crossed out.

- The circled numbers are the prime numbers between 1 and 100.

- Write out the prime numbers between 1 and 100.

_____

_____

# The Sieve of Eratosthenes

This method of finding all the prime numbers between 0 and 100 is called the Sieve of Eratosthenes because it lets all the composite numbers go through and holds on to the prime numbers.

1. See if you can answer these questions.

   (a) How many prime numbers between 1 and 100? _____

   (b) Which is the lowest prime number? _____

   (c) Which prime number is nearest to 100? _____

   (d) Is 91 a prime number? _____ Explain.
       (Because the factors of 91 are _____, _____, _____, _____)

   (e) 3 and 5 are called twin primes because there is a difference of 2 between them.
       Write 7 other sets of twin primes.

   _____, _____, _____, _____, _____, _____, _____

   (f) Are there any prime numbers with a difference of 1? _____

   (g) How many pairs of prime numbers with a difference of 10 are there in the hundred square? _____

   (h) Name the one and only prime number that is also an even number. _____

   (i) What kind of number do you get when you add 2 prime numbers? _____

   (j) Find the missing fraction:

       [ __ ] of the numbers between 1 and 100 are prime numbers.

## Prime Time

Each letter below is followed by a number. Cross out each composite number and its letter. Write down the letters that are left in the space below.
Then read across and you should find the name of a famous song.

| L21 | R36 | A11 | W7 | P48 | H31 | S24 | I19 | N18 | T13 | E19 |

| V60 | R28 | C41 | P50 | H43 | R59 | C65 | I71 | S89 | P91 | Q98 | T47 | M97 | A61 | S53 |

1. Find the sum of these three numbers: 876, 74 and 7974. _____

2. Take 796 from 1200. _____

3. Find the number that is 16 smaller than 400. _____

4. Find the cost of 15 football jerseys at €25 each. _____

5. Michael spent $1\frac{1}{2}$ hours at his homework last night.
   He spent $\frac{2}{5}$ of that time doing mathematics.
   How many minutes did he spend at mathematics? _____

6. By how much is 16.2 bigger than 9.75? _____

7. Find the length of the perimeter
   of this triangle._____

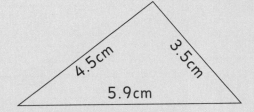

4.5cm   3.5cm   5.9cm

8. How many centimetres in 2m 70cm? _____

9. How many metres in $3\frac{1}{2}$ km? _____

10. Write 3m 96cm as metres in decimal form._____

11. Change 8765 metres to kilometres and metres._____

12. With your protractor,
    measure the size of the angle
    between the hands of this clock _____

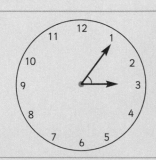

13. Draw an angle of 75° in this box.

# Time to look back 3

14. Without using a protractor, find the measure of the angle marked C in this triangle. _____

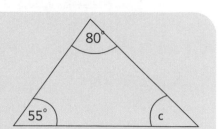

15. Put a tick (✓) in the box beside the equilateral triangle.

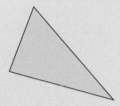  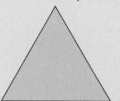  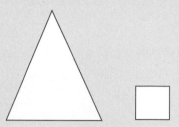

16. Draw a diameter in this circle.

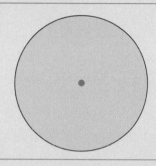

17. One of the factors of 12 is missing. Can you fill it in?

F12 = (1, 2, 3, 4, ____ ,12)

18. All the prime numbers between 21 and 40, except one, are coloured in this part of the 100 square. Can you colour in the missing one?

| 21 | 22 | 23 | 24 | 25 | 26 | 27 | 28 | 29 | 30 |
| 31 | 32 | 33 | 34 | 35 | 36 | 37 | 38 | 39 | 40 |

19. Colour the quadrilaterals in this tangram.

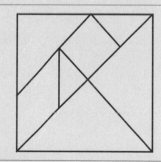

20. Colour in the composite numbers on this strip.

| 16 | 17 | 18 | 19 | 20 | 21 | 22 | 23 |

How well did you do? Tick the box that shows your score.

18 – 20
Excellent

15 – 17
Very good

10 – 14
Good

0 – 9
Keep up the good work

# Chapter 15
## Fractions 2

**You need:**
- colouring pencils
- to explain numerator, denominator, improper fractions and mixed numbers

## A Looking back

1. True or false?

|  | | True | False |
|---|---|---|---|
| (a) | Fifty cent is half a euro. | ☐ | ☐ |
| (b) | Ten hours is a quarter of a day. | ☐ | ☐ |
| (c) | Twenty-five cent is three quarters of a euro. | ☐ | ☐ |
| (d) | A day is one seventh of a week. | ☐ | ☐ |
| (e) | Five eighths is bigger than a half. | ☐ | ☐ |
| (f) | Seventy-five centimetres is one tenth of a metre. | ☐ | ☐ |
| (g) | Half is less than a sixth. | ☐ | ☐ |
| (h) | Six is two thirds of nine. | ☐ | ☐ |
| (i) | Six twelfths is the same as a half. | ☐ | ☐ |
| (j) | Eight hours is one third of a day. | ☐ | ☐ |

2. Put a tick (✓) or an (✗) in the boxes to show which of these is correct.

(a) $\frac{1}{2} = \frac{3}{4}$ ☐  (b) $\frac{2}{5} = \frac{1}{10}$ ☐  (c) $\frac{1}{3} = \frac{2}{6}$ ☐  (d) $\frac{3}{6} = \frac{1}{2}$ ☐  (e) $\frac{7}{8} = \frac{1}{2}$ ☐

(f) $\frac{3}{4} = \frac{7}{8}$ ☐  (g) $\frac{1}{2} = \frac{5}{10}$ ☐  (h) $\frac{1}{2} = \frac{2}{4}$ ☐  (i) $\frac{3}{9} = \frac{1}{3}$ ☐  (j) $\frac{9}{12} = \frac{3}{4}$ ☐

3. Colour the correct amounts.

(a)

$\frac{1}{4}$ pink,
$\frac{3}{4}$ yellow

(b)

$\frac{1}{2}$ red,
$\frac{1}{4}$ green, $\frac{1}{4}$ blue

(c)
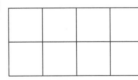
$\frac{1}{8}$ red, $\frac{7}{8}$ green

(d)
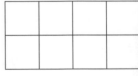
$\frac{1}{2}$ yellow, $\frac{3}{8}$ red,
$\frac{1}{8}$ blue

(e)

$\frac{1}{4}$ red, $\frac{1}{2}$ blue
$\frac{1}{8}$ pink, $\frac{1}{8}$ green

(f)

$\frac{1}{3}$ red, $\frac{2}{3}$ blue

(g)
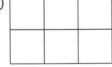
$\frac{1}{6}$ blue, $\frac{1}{6}$ yellow,
$\frac{1}{3}$ red, $\frac{1}{3}$ green

(h)

$\frac{5}{10}$ green, $\frac{3}{10}$ blue, $\frac{1}{5}$ yellow

(i)
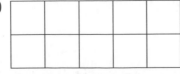
$\frac{1}{10}$ blue, $\frac{1}{2}$ red, $\frac{2}{5}$ green

(j)

$\frac{1}{3}$ red, $\frac{1}{6}$ green, $\frac{1}{2}$ blue

# Numerator and denominator

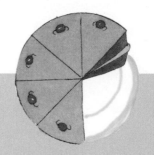

There are $\frac{5}{8}$ of a cake on this plate.

$$\text{denominator} \longrightarrow \frac{5}{8} \longleftarrow \text{numerator}$$

The word 'denominator' comes from the Latin word 'nomen', which means name.
In this fraction the parts are named eighths and there are eight parts in the full cake.

The word 'numerator' comes from the Latin word 'numerus', which means number.
The 5 in this fraction tells us that there are five of the eight parts on the plate.

This time we have 7 markers out of a full set of ten.

$\frac{7}{10}$   = numerator ➤ number of markers = 7
   = denominator ➤ name of parts = tenths.

We have seven of the ten markers in the set.

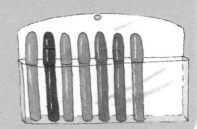

1. Fill in the missing numerators in these pairs of fractions.

(a)   $\frac{1}{2} = \frac{}{4}$

(b)   $\frac{5}{6} = \frac{}{12}$

(c)   $\frac{3}{4} = \frac{}{12}$

(d)   $\frac{2}{3} = \frac{}{9}$

(e)   $\frac{2}{5} = \frac{}{10}$

(f)   $\frac{4}{5} = \frac{}{10}$

(g)   $\frac{1}{3} = \frac{}{12}$

(h)   $\frac{1}{2} = \frac{}{10}$

(i)   $\frac{}{6} = \frac{1}{2}$

(j)   $\frac{2}{8} = \frac{}{4}$

(k)   $\frac{}{12} = \frac{1}{2}$

(l)   $\frac{1}{3} = \frac{}{6}$

2. Fill in the missing denominators in these pairs of fractions.

(a)   $\frac{1}{3} = \frac{3}{}$

(b)   $\frac{1}{5} = \frac{2}{}$

(c)   $\frac{6}{9} = \frac{2}{}$

(d)   $\frac{6}{10} = \frac{3}{}$

(e)   $\frac{1}{2} = \frac{4}{}$

(f)   $\frac{1}{4} = \frac{3}{}$

(g)   $\frac{5}{6} = \frac{10}{}$

(h)   $\frac{5}{} = \frac{1}{2}$

(i)   $\frac{4}{6} = \frac{}{3}$

(j)   $\frac{4}{4} = \frac{}{6}$

(k)   $\frac{}{6} = \frac{12}{12}$

(l)   $\frac{}{6} = \frac{}{7}$

# Improper fractions and mixed numbers

**B Moving on**

$\frac{5}{9}$ is a proper fraction – the numerator is **<u>less</u>** than the denominator.

$\frac{16}{9}$ is an improper fraction – the numerator is **<u>greater</u>** than the denominator.

$1\frac{7}{9}$ is a mixed number – a whole number and a fraction.

**Example 1**

How many half sandwiches? $\frac{1}{2} + \frac{1}{2} + \frac{1}{2} + \frac{1}{2} + \frac{1}{2} = \frac{5}{2}$ (Five halves)
This is an **improper fraction**.

How many sandwiches? $(\frac{1}{2} + \frac{1}{2}) + (\frac{1}{2} + \frac{1}{2}) + \frac{1}{2} = \frac{5}{2} = 2\frac{1}{2}$
This is a **mixed number.**

**Example 2**

How many quarters?
$\frac{11}{4}$ is an improper fraction.

$\frac{1}{4} + \frac{1}{4} + \frac{1}{4} + \frac{1}{4} + \frac{1}{4} + \frac{1}{4} + \frac{1}{4} + \frac{1}{4} + \frac{1}{4} + \frac{1}{4} + \frac{1}{4} = \frac{11}{4}$

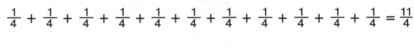

How many pizzas? $(\frac{1}{4} + \frac{1}{4} + \frac{1}{4} + \frac{1}{4}) + (\frac{1}{4} + \frac{1}{4} + \frac{1}{4} + \frac{1}{4}) + \frac{1}{4} + \frac{1}{4} + \frac{1}{4} = \frac{11}{4} = 2\frac{3}{4}$
$2\frac{3}{4}$ is a mixed number.

**Example 3**

These 25 markers are to be sold in sets of 10.
Each marker is $\frac{1}{10}$ of a set.

How many tenths? $\boxed{\phantom{-}}$

How many sets? $\underline{\phantom{-}}\,\boxed{\phantom{-}}$

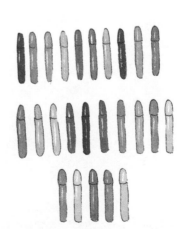

# Rewriting improper fractions as mixed numbers

**Example**

(a) $\frac{9}{6} = \frac{6}{6} + \frac{3}{6} = 1\frac{3}{6} = 1\frac{1}{2}$

(b) $\frac{12}{5} = \boxed{\frac{5}{5}} + \boxed{\frac{5}{5}} + \boxed{\frac{}{5}} = \boxed{\phantom{\frac{}{}}}$

Now try these.

1. (a) $\frac{3}{2} = $ _____
   (b) $\frac{7}{4} = $ _____
   (c) $\frac{10}{3} = $ _____
   (d) $\frac{5}{2} = $ _____

2. (a) $\frac{11}{5} = $ _____
   (b) $\frac{14}{6} = $ _____
   (c) $\frac{9}{7} = $ _____
   (d) $\frac{9}{6} = $ _____

3. (a) $\frac{22}{10} = $ _____
   (b) $\frac{20}{8} = $ _____
   (c) $\frac{24}{11} = $ _____
   (d) $\frac{15}{9} = $ _____

4. (a) $\frac{21}{9} = $ _____
   (b) $\frac{25}{6} = $ _____
   (c) $\frac{28}{12} = $ _____
   (d) $\frac{15}{7} = $ _____

## Rewriting mixed numbers as improper fractions

**Example 1**

$2\frac{2}{5} = 1 + 1 + \frac{2}{5} = \frac{5}{5} + \frac{5}{5} + \frac{2}{5} = \frac{12}{5}$

**Example 2**

$3\frac{1}{2} = 1 + 1 + 1 + \frac{1}{2} = \frac{2}{2} + \frac{2}{2} + \frac{2}{2} + \frac{2}{2} = \boxed{\frac{}{2}}$

1. Rewrite these mixed numbers as improper fractions

(a) $1\frac{1}{2} = \boxed{\phantom{\frac{}{}}}$
(b) $2\frac{1}{3} = \boxed{\phantom{\frac{}{}}}$
(c) $3\frac{1}{4} = \boxed{\phantom{\frac{}{}}}$
(d) $1\frac{6}{7} = \boxed{\phantom{\frac{}{}}}$

(e) $3\frac{3}{8} = \boxed{\phantom{\frac{}{}}}$
(f) $2\frac{4}{9} = \boxed{\phantom{\frac{}{}}}$
(g) $2\frac{4}{11} = \boxed{\phantom{\frac{}{}}}$
(h) $3\frac{3}{10} = \boxed{\phantom{\frac{}{}}}$

(i) $4\frac{5}{12} = \boxed{\phantom{\frac{}{}}}$
(j) $3\frac{5}{6} = \boxed{\phantom{\frac{}{}}}$
(k) $2\frac{2}{5} = \boxed{\phantom{\frac{}{}}}$
(l) $2\frac{4}{9} = \boxed{\phantom{\frac{}{}}}$

2. Write the answers to these questions as mixed numbers.

(a) How many bunches of eight flowers can be made from 26 flowers? _____

(b) This packet contains 10 sweets.
    How many packets can be made from 35 sweets? _____

# Fractions on the number line

1. Fill in the missing improper fractions on these number lines.

(a)
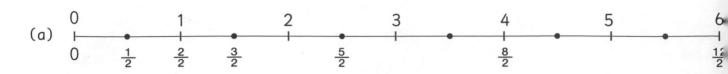

(b)
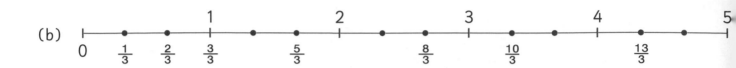

(c)

(d)
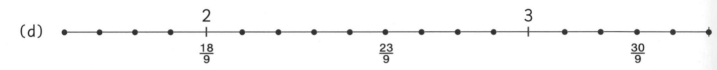

2. Fill in the missing mixed numbers on these number lines.

(a)

(b)
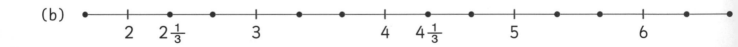

(c)

3. Fill in the missing mixed numbers above the line, and the missing improper fractions below the line.

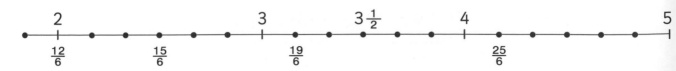

# Problems for you to solve

Write your answers as mixed numbers with the fraction in its **simplest form**,

e.g. $2\frac{2}{4} = 2\frac{1}{2}$

1. Packets of crisps are sold in large packs of 10.
   How many large packs can be made from 45 packets?_____

2. Apples are sold in bags of 8.
   How many bags can be filled from 78 apples?_____

3. Yogurts are sold in packs of 4.
   How many packs can be made from 99 yogurts?_____

4. These bottles of water are packed in sixes for sale.
   How many packs of six can be made from 58 bottles of water?_____

5. Bars are sold in packs of ten.
   How many packs can be made from 96 bars?_____

## And now a challenge ...

Three quarters of the mixed numbers in Set A have a matching equivalent improper fraction in Set B. Can you find the matching pairs?
You score 2 points for every correct pair you find. Write the pairs on the lines below.

**Set A**

$1\frac{6}{9}$    $4\frac{7}{12}$    $2\frac{1}{2}$    $6\frac{1}{4}$    $7\frac{3}{5}$    $3\frac{1}{11}$    $5\frac{2}{3}$    $4\frac{1}{5}$    $1\frac{3}{4}$    $7\frac{7}{10}$    $6\frac{2}{3}$    $4\frac{5}{6}$

**Set B**

$\frac{50}{8}$    $\frac{21}{5}$    $\frac{29}{6}$    $\frac{7}{4}$    $\frac{10}{4}$    $\frac{40}{5}$    $\frac{78}{10}$    $\frac{15}{9}$    $\frac{34}{6}$    $\frac{55}{12}$    $\frac{34}{11}$    $\frac{21}{3}$

_____

_____

I found _____ pairs.    I scored [    ]

**You need:**
- a calculator
- to revise rounding

**A Looking back**

# Multiplication of decimals

1. This teacher, Ms Smart, was shopping for prizes for a charity raffle in her school. First she bought 3 books at €11.75 each. How much did she pay for the books?

   3 x €11.75

   €11.75   2 decimal places
   x3
   **€35.25**   2 decimal places

   Calculator  `1` `1` `·` `7` `5` `X` `3`
   `=` **35.25**

2. Ms Smart then bought 5 CDs costing €15.99 each. How much did she spend on CDs?

   5 x €15.99

   €15.99   2 decimal places
   x5
   € _ _ . _ _   2 decimal places

   Calculator  `1` `5` `·` `9` `9` `X` `5`
   `=` _ _ . _ _

3. Now try these. Check your answers using a calculator.

   (a) €16.95   (b) €12.36   (c) €24.15   (d) €29.27   (e) €35.67
       x4           x6           x8           x9           x7

4. Do these in your copy and check the answers using a calculator.

   (a) 7 x €36.99    (b) 8 x €45.57    (c) 10 x €51.82   (d) 9 x €65.09
   (e) 5 x €27.36    (f) 6 x €72.65    (g) 8 x €75.75    (h) 10 x €78.99

5. This time use your calculator to find the answers.

   (a) 5 x 95.6 _____     (b) 7 x 68.75 _____    (c) 6 x 84.35 _____

   (d) 10 x 67.59 _____   (e) 8 x 96.27 _____    (f) 9 x 72.98 _____

   (g) 6 x 95.64 _____    (h) 9 x 68.2 _____     (i) 8 x 59.45 _____

   (j) 8 x 86.27 _____    (k) 7 x 84.95 _____    (l) 10 x 96.5 _____

   (m) 5 x 100.35 _____   (n) 6 x 126.35 _____   (o) 7 x 184.96 _____

# Multiplication of decimals

1. Ms Smart went to a supermarket and bought 4 boxes of biscuits as prizes. Each box weighed 1.375kg. What was the total weight?

   4 x 1.375kg

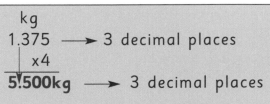

   kg
   1.375 ——→ 3 decimal places
        x4
   5.500kg ——→ 3 decimal places

   Calculator `1` `.` `3` `7` `5` `X` `4`
                `=` 5.5

2. Finally, Ms Smart needed two very large boxes of chocolates. Each box contained 1.555kg of chocolates. Find the total weight of the chocolates.

   2 x 1.555kg

   kg
   1.555 ——→ 3 decimal places
        x2
   _._ _ _kg ——→ 3 decimal places

   Calculator ☐ `.` ☐ ☐ ☐ `X` ☐
                `=` __.__ __ __

3. Now try these. Use a calculator to check your answers.

   (a)    2.705        (b)    6.654        (c)    9.625        (d)    7.825
            x4                  x5                  x6                  x10

4. Do these in your copy and check your answers using a calculator.

   (a)  2 x 5.126        (b)  4 x 7.345        (c)  3 x 6.755        (d)  6 x 3.569
   (e)  5 x 8.705        (f)  7 x 9.006        (g)  10 x 7.125       (h)  6 x 19.345
   (i)  9 x 12.305       (j)  8 x 18.125       (k)  4 x 27.125       (l)  8 x 14.625

5. Use your calculator to find the answers.

   (a) 6 x 39.625 = _____        (b)  8 x 96.125 = _____        (c)  3 x 75.603 = _____

   (d) 10 x 27.555 = _____       (e)  7 x 84.999 = _____        (f)  4 x 90.008 = _____

   (g) 9 x 68.004 = _____        (h)  8 x 88.888 = _____        (i)  5 x 50.505 = _____

# Long multiplication of decimals

1. This group of 48 fifth class children won a visit to this restaurant in a school competition. Twenty-three of the children chose a meal priced €5.99.

   How much did the 23 meals cost?

   23 x €5.99

   €5.99 ——► 2 decimal places
   x23

   3x€5.99 ——► 17¦97
   20x€5.99 ——►119¦80

   €137.77 ——►2 decimal places

   Calculator [5][·][9][9][X][2][3]

   [=] 137.77

2. The remaining 25 children in the group each had a meal costing €6.25. How much did their meals cost?

   25 x €6.25

   6.25 ——►2 decimal places
   x25

   5x€6.25 ► _ _ _ _
   20x€6.25 ► _ _ _ _ _

   € _ _ _ _ . _ _ ——►2 decimal places

   Calculator [ ][ ][ ][ ][X][ ][ ]

   [=] _ _ _ _ . _ _

3. Work out the answers and then check using a calculator.

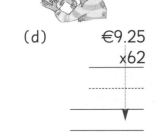

   (a)        €3.95
              x35
   --------------------

              ▼
   _____

   (b)        €7.39
              x45
   --------------------

              ▼
   _____

   (c)        €8.75
              x56
   --------------------

              ▼
   _____

   (d)        €9.25
              x62
   --------------------

              ▼
   _____

4. Do these questions in your copy and check your answers using a calculator.
   (a) 12 x 24.54 _____
   (b) 14 x 36.93 _____
   (c) 18 x 45.32 _____
   (d) 23 x 19.65 _____
   (e) 39 x 12.27 _____
   (f) 42 x 16.75 _____
   (g) 56 x 25.92 _____
   (h) 65 x 36.04 _____
   (i) 72 x 45.08 _____
   (j) 86 x 50.62 _____
   (k) 91 x 75.15 _____
   (l) 99 x 50.12 _____
   (m) 74 x 42.64 _____
   (n) 93 x 59.63 _____
   (o) 87 x 92.75 _____

# Long multiplication of decimals – again

1. This man is delivering 15 containers of mayonnaise to the restaurant. Each container weighs 2.625kg.

   What is the total weight of the mayonnaise?

   15 x 2.625kg

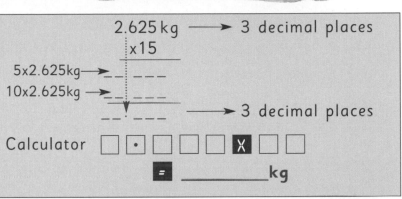

2. Twenty-three boxes of burgers, each weighing 4.125kg, were also delivered to the restaurant. Find the total weight of the boxes.

   23 x 4.125kg

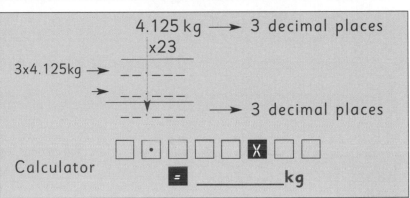

3. Work out the answers in your copy and check your work using a calculator.

   (a) 25 x 4.125     (b) 36 x 1.705     (c) 45 x 9.004
   (d) 56 x 5.075     (e) 63 x 9.072     (f) 37 x 8.705
   (g) 26 x 25.126    (h) 48 x 12.365    (i) 55 x 52.625
   (j) 72 x 32.255    (k) 61 x 23.135    (l) 80 x 45.125

4. This time use your calculator to find the answers.

   (a) 54 x 96.175_____     (b) 36 x 87.875_____     (c) 27 x 65.625_____

   (d) 76 x 85.125_____     (e) 65 x 39.009_____     (f) 58 x 74.025_____

   (g) 89 x 89.089_____     (h) 93 x 62.825_____     (i) 99 x 56.987_____

# Shopping!

These are some of the things Brian and his Dad bought in the supermarket.

1.   Find the weight of

     (a) two bags of potatoes each weighing 6.35kg                                   _____kg

     (b) 6 bananas if each banana weighs approximately 0.15kg                         _____kg

     (c) 4 cans of beans each weighing 0.435kg                                        _____kg

     (d) a bag of 12 apples if each apple weighs approximately 0.175kg               _____kg

     (e) Use a calculator to find the total weight of the groceries.                 _____kg

2.   A bag of potatoes is —————kg heavier than 24 apples.

3.   Six bananas are —————kg lighter than 6 apples.

4.   12 apples are _____ kg heavier than 12 bananas.

5.   2 cans of beans are _____ kg lighter than 6 bananas.

6.   Which is heavier: a bag of potatoes or 10 cans of beans? _____

Check your answers using a calculator.

## Magic!

Using a calculator to multiply decimals by 10.

(a) Start ———→    1.234
    x 10  ———→    12.34
    x 10  ———→    123.4
    x 10  ———→    1234

(b) Start ———→    5.678
    x 10  ———→
    x 10  ———→
    x 10  ———→

(c) Now try
    Start ———→    1.008
    x 10  ———→
    x 10  ———→
    x 10  ———→

(d) What do you notice?
    When you multiply a decimal by ten _____

    _____

    _____

    _____

# Division of decimals

**Example 1**

Divide this chocolate equally between 2 children.

 = 2½ bars = 2.5 bars of chocolate.

  = 1¼ = 1.25

 = 1¼ = 1.25

They each get 1.25 bars of chocolate.

$$2.5 \div 2 = \quad 2\overline{|2.5^1 0}$$
$$\overline{1\;25}$$

**Example 2**

Divide this chocolate equally between 8 children.

 = 3 bars of chocolate

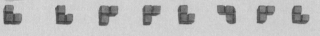  Each child gets $\frac{3}{8}$ of a bar

$$3 \div 8 = 8\overline{|3.0^3 0^6 0^4}$$
$$0.375 = \frac{3}{8}$$

1. Now try these and check your answers using a calculator.

    (a) $2\overline{|2.5}$     (b) $5\overline{|4.75}$     (c) $4\overline{|8.24}$     (d) $6\overline{|7.08}$     (e) $8\overline{|17.608}$

2. Do this question and check your answer using a calculator.
   Divide €12.54 equally among 6 children.

   $6\overline{|€12.54}$
   €___ . ___ ___

   Calculator  = ___ . ___ ___

3. Do these questions in your copy and check your answers using a calculator.

    (a) €48.32 ÷ 2     (b) €39.00 ÷ 4     (c) €98.72 ÷ 8
    (d) €80.92 ÷ 7     (e) €74.88 ÷ 9     (f) €124.02 ÷ 3
    (g) €152.88 ÷ 6     (h) €48.75 ÷ 5     (i) €114.75 ÷ 9

4. Now try these.

    (a) €53.00 ÷ 4 = _____     (b) €91.75 ÷ 5 = _____     (c) €74.00 ÷ 8 = _____
    (d) €85.33 ÷ 7 = _____     (e) €115.75 ÷ 5 = _____     (f) €136.80 ÷ 6 = _____
    (g) $3\overline{|15.705km}$     (h) $6\overline{|43.452l}$     (i) $8\overline{|206.48kg}$

    _____        _____        _____

# Long division of decimals

1. The two fifth classes from this school went out for a day.

   (a) One of the fifth classes had 27 pupils.
   The teacher collected €587.25 for the day out.
   How much did each pupil pay?

   Calculator 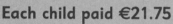 21.75
   **Each child paid €21.75**

   ```
           €21.75
   27 | €587.25
       -54
        47
       -27
       2Ø2
      -189
        135
        135
          0
   ```

   (b) The 25 pupils in the second fifth class spent €260.75 during the day out.
   What was the average amount spent? €260.75 ÷ 25
   The average amount spent per pupil = _____

   (c) Check your answer using a calculator.

   ```
        €  _ _ . _ _
   25 |€ 2 6 0 . 7 5
   ```

2. Work out the answers in your copy and check using a calculator.

   (a) 73.64 ÷ 14      (b) 108.45 ÷ 15      (c) 225.72 ÷ 22      (d) 190.75 ÷ 35
   (e) 127.44 ÷ 24      (f) 281.25 ÷ 45      (g) 388.96 ÷ 52      (h) 289.68 ÷ 68

3. Now use your calculator to find the answers.

   (a) 154.56 ÷ 23 = _____      (b) 537.6 ÷ 35 = _____      (c) 734.28 ÷ 29 = _____

   (d) 636.96 ÷ 48 = _____      (e) 662.58 ÷ 54 = _____      (f) 536.5 ÷ 58 = _____

   (g) 654.1 ÷ 62 = _____      (h) 857.5 ÷ 70 = _____      (i) 329.4 ÷ 45 = _____

   (j) 467.5 ÷ 55 = _____      (k) 456.03 ÷ 81 = _____      (l) 446.25 ÷ 85 = _____

   (m) 2568.6km ÷ 36 = _____      (n) 689.92kg ÷ 44 = _____      (o) 391.5l ÷ 29 = _____

# Problems for you to solve

1.  This man drives to and from work at this motor factory five days a week.

    (a) If he travels 71.25km driving to and from work every week, how far is his house from the factory? _____k m

    (b) He earns €507.20 per week.
        How much does he earn per day? _____

    (c) He saves €35 every week.
        How long will it take to save enough to buy a
        computer for €612.50 ? _____

    (d) He works an eight-hour day.
        How much is he paid per hour? _____

    (e) The box he is carrying weighs 16.175kg and contains 5 CD
        players for the new cars.
        How much does each CD player weigh? _____ kg

## Magic!

Using a calculator to divide a decimal by 10.

(a) Start ──────▶      123.4
    ÷ 10 ──────▶      12.34
    ÷ 10 ──────▶      1.234
    ÷ 10 ──────▶      0.1 234

(b)   Your turn!
      Start ──────▶      567.8
      ÷ 10 ──────▶
      ÷ 10 ──────▶
      ÷ 10 ──────▶

What do you notice?
When you divide a decimal by ten_____
_____
_____
_____

(c) Now try this one.
    Start ──────▶      100.5
    ÷ 10 ──────▶
    ÷ 10 ──────▶
    ÷ 10 ──────▶

# Rounding decimals to the nearest whole number

To round decimals to the nearest whole number you need to look at the digit in the tenths' place.

1. Fill in the missing numbers on this part of the number line.

5 ___ 5.2 ___ ___ 5.5 ___ ___ 5.8 ___ 6

**Example 1**
Round 5.2 to the nearest whole number.
5.2 is nearer to 5.0 than to 6.
5.2 rounds down to 5.

**Example 2**
Round 5.5 to the nearest whole number.
5.5 is half way between 5 and 6.
Numbers containing .5 or bigger round up.
5.5 rounds up to 6.

2. Round these numbers up or down to the nearest whole number.

(a) 9.8 _____ (b) 4.5 _____ (c) 22.2 _____ (d) 19.1 _____

(e) 36.3 _____ (f) 99.6 _____ (g) 27.9 _____ (h) 75.4 _____

(i) 87.2 _____ (j) 100.8 _____ (k) 289.7 _____ (l) 501.2 _____

55.**5** rounds up to 56.
36.**3**75 rounds down to 36.

Look at the digit in the tenths' place!

3. Round these numbers to the nearest whole number.

(a) 12.27 _____ (b) 29.98 _____ (c) 37.09 _____ (d) 48.68 _____

(e) 48.285 _____ (f) 59.675 _____ (g) 63.028 _____ (h) 96.709 _____

(i) 106.875 _____ (j) 275.005 _____ (k) 409.725 _____ (l) 610.215 _____

**Example 3**
Rounding helps us in estimation.

|  | Rounding | Estimate | Exact answer |
| --- | --- | --- | --- |
| (a) 25 x 3.9 | 25 x 4 | 100 | 97.5 |
| (b) 15.8 ÷ 4 | 16 ÷ 4 | 4 | 3.95 |

4. Round the decimals, estimate and then use a calculator to find the exact answer.

|  | Rounding | Estimate | Exact answer |
| --- | --- | --- | --- |
| (a) 37.125 + 89.56 | _____ | _____ | _____ |
| (b) 124.652 – 23.25 | _____ | _____ | _____ |
| (c) 25 x 3.9 | _____ | _____ | _____ |
| (d) 76 x 5.1 | _____ | _____ | _____ |
| (e) 59.6 ÷ 4 | _____ | _____ | _____ |
| (f) 90.36 ÷ 6 | | | |

# A mixed bag of decimals

Choose the correct number from the bag to fill the blanks in these sequences.

1. (a) 3.4, _____ , 3.6
   (c) 3.207, _____ , 3.209
   (e) 3.29, _____ , 3.31
   (b) 3.51, _____ , 3.53
   (d) 3.9, _____ , 4.1
   (f) 3.189, _____ , 3.191

2. (a) 5.5, _____ , 5.7
   (c) 5.127, _____ , 5.129
   (e) 5.49, _____ , 5.51
   (b) 5.25, _____ , 5.27
   (d) 5.8, _____ , 6.0
   (f) 5.139, _____ , 5.141

3. (a) 29.2, _____ , 29.4
   (c) 29.125, _____ , 29.127
   (e) 29.09, _____ , 29.11
   (b) 29.16, _____ , 29.18
   (d) 29.9, _____ , 30.1
   (f) 29.198, _____ , 29.2

4. You may use a calculator to check the answers to these questions.

   (a) 9999.999 + 0.001 =     My guess: _____     Exact answer: _____

   (b) 8020.099 + 0.001 =     My guess: _____     Exact answer: _____

   (c) 10 000.909 + 0.001 =     My guess: _____     Exact answer: _____

   (d) 9009.098 + 0.002 =     My guess: _____     Exact answer: _____

# Go for it!

Where possible, check your answers using a calculator.

1. 1475g = _____kg  +  $\boxed{\frac{}{10}}$ + $\boxed{\frac{}{100}}$ + $\boxed{\frac{}{1000}}$ = ____._____ kg

2. 13 086g =_____kg  +  $\boxed{\frac{}{10}}$ + $\boxed{\frac{}{100}}$ + $\boxed{\frac{}{1000}}$ = ____._____ kg

3. Put these decimals in order starting with the largest.

   6.01      6.175      6.9      6.35      6.04      6.2

   _____   _____   _____   _____   _____   _____

4. Put these decimals in order starting with the smallest.

   25.75    25.625    25.005    25.55    25.125    25.5

   _____   _____   _____   _____   _____   _____

5. 9.05 + 304.5 + 17.875 = _____

6. 5.125 + 26.05 + 1250.9 + 268.009 = _____

7. 130.125 – 68.75 = _____

8. 142.625 – 19.599 = _____

9. 36 x 217.35 = _____

10. 50 x 125.75 = _____

11. 125.875 ÷ 25 = _____

12. 603 ÷ 36 = _____

A marathon is 42.195km in length!

13. (a) James ran the following distances over three days in preparation for a marathon: 22.175km, 29.875km and 37.5km. How many kilometres is that in total?_____

   (b) Siobhán had to drop out of the marathon when she injured her ankle, having completed $\frac{3}{5}$ of the race.
   How far had she run by then? _____

   (c) Ciaran took a drink of water when he had completed $\frac{1}{5}$ of the marathon. How far was he from the finish line when he took a drink of water? _____

   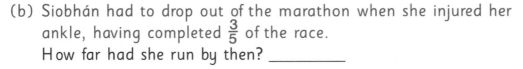

   (d) Siobhán has completed 11 marathons.
   What distance has she run in marathons so far? _____

   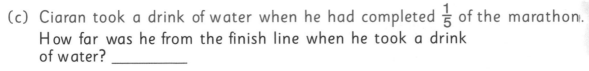

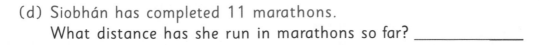

# Chapter 17

## Weight

**You need:**
- a calculator — the items for Q1
- a bathroom scales   on page 110
- a kitchen scales

We use kilogrammes and grammes to weigh things.

 1kg = 1000g

A bag of sugar weighs 1kg.     A spoonful of sugar weighs about 1g.

1. Would you use kilogrammes or grammes to measure the following items?
   Tick the correct one.

| | Item | kg | g |
|---|---|---|---|
| 1 | Potatoes | | |
| 2 | Biscuits | | |
| 3 | Cornflakes | | |
| 4 | Coal | | |
| 5 | A newborn baby | | |
| 6 | Luggage bag | | |
| 7 | A Christmas cake | | |
| 8 | Turkey | | |
| 9 | Jar of coffee | | |
| 10 | Packet of sweets | | |

2. Put these items in order starting with the lightest.

   (a) bicycle  (b) kettle  (c) pencil  (d) lorry  (e) spoon  (f) plane
   (g) chair    (h) CD      (i) car     (j) washing machine

   _____   _____   _____   _____   _____

   _____   _____   _____   _____   _____

# Estimate and weigh

1. Your teacher will find the 6 items listed in the table below.
   Estimate their weight in grammes. Keep your estimate to the
   nearest 100g and write it in the table below.
   Then each item will be weighed on the kitchen scales.

| | | Estimate | Exact Weight | Difference |
|---|---|---|---|---|
| 1 | Maths Matters 5 | g | g | g |
| 2 | Glassful of water | g | g | g |
| 3 | School bell | g | g | g |
| 4 | An orange | g | g | g |
| 5 | 3 paintbrushes | g | g | g |
| 6 | 2 Maths copies | g | g | g |

How accurate was your estimate? _____

2. Write out the six weights in order starting with the heaviest.

   _____

3. Now with your calculator find out the total exact weight of all
   the items. Then find the total difference between your
   estimate and the exact answer.

   Total estimate weight:_____kg _____g
   Total exact weight:_____kg _____g
   Total difference:_____kg _____g

   To show 3kg 495g
   on your calculator
   key in 3.495

4. Find the average weight of the 6 items by
   dividing the total exact weight by 6. _____
   Check your answer with your calculator.

5. The difference between the average weight
   and the heaviest item is _____

6. The difference between the lightest item
   and the average weight is _____

7. Name the items which are

   (a) above the average weight:

   _____

   (b) below the average weight:

   _____

110

# Weigh-in time

Look at the weights of these three children and answer the following questions.

(a) Who is the heaviest? _____

(b) Who is the lightest? _____

(c) What is the difference between their weights? _____

(d) Find the total weight of the three children. _____

(e) Now find the average weight. _____

(f) How many of the children are above the average weight? _____

(g) Who is below the average weight? _____

(h) Round the average weight to the nearest kg. _____

(i) Round each of the children's weights to the nearest kg.

Martin _____          Niamh _____          Graham _____

(j) Here is a line graph of the rounded weights and the rounded average weight of the three children.

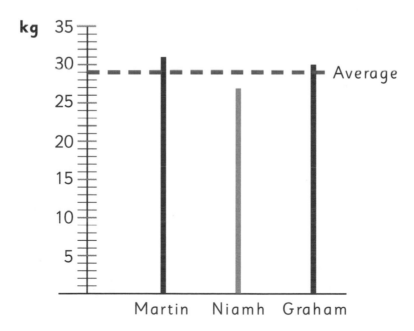

(k) Discuss it with your friend or partner.

# Weigh-in time 2

This table shows the names and weights of a group of 20 schoolchildren.

|  | kg |  | kg |  | kg |  | kg |
|---|---|---|---|---|---|---|---|
| Sarah | 27.126 | Aisling | 29.58 | Paul | 30.126 | Shane | 31.286 |
| Stacey | 31.955 | Ruth | 31.75 | Michael | 29.545 | Colm | 34.5 |
| Fiona | 25.684 | Jennifer | 32.975 | Karl | 31.758 | Danny | 30.98 |
| Nicola | 30.55 | Shauna | 30.915 | James | 28.35 | Ivan | 32.525 |
| Julie | 27.6 | Áine | 27.372 | John | 32.875 | Matthew | 29.925 |

Use this data and your calculator, where you can, to answer the following questions.

(a) Who is the heaviest in the group? _____

(b) Who is the lightest in the group? _____

(c) What is the difference between their weights? _____

(d) Find the total weight of the girls. _____

(e) Round the girls' total weight to the nearest kg. _____

(f) Use that rounded total girls' weight to find the average weight of the girls to the nearest kg. _____

(g) Find the total weight of the boys. _____

(h) Round that total weight to the nearest kg. _____

(i) Use the rounded total boys' weight to find the average weight for the boys to the nearest kg. _____

(j) Now, in your copy, using the children's rounded weights, draw two line graphs. The first graph will show the girls' weights and the second graph will show the boys' weights. Don't forget to show the average weight on both graphs.

(k) How many boys are above the average boys' weight? _____

(l) How many boys are below the average boys' weight? _____

(m) How many girls are above the average girls' weight? _____

(n) How many girls are below the average girls' weight? _____

# Problems for you to solve

You can use your calculator to find the answers.
Here is an example to help you.

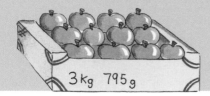

1. A shopkeeper bought 25kg of carrots at €1.50 per kg.
   He sold them in bags of 500g at €1.29 per bag.
   How much profit did he make? _____

2. A butcher sold 2 turkeys a few days before Christmas. One turkey
   weighed $8\frac{1}{2}$ kg and the other weighed 7kg.
   He sold them at €3.90 per kg.
   How much money did he get altogether for the 2 turkeys? _____

3. A packet of 12 whiteboard markers weighs 225g.
   They are packed in cardboard boxes which can hold 48 packets.
   What is the total weight of 2 full boxes? _____
   (Allow 150g for each box when empty.)

4. The Molloy family are packing to go on holiday.
   They have a baggage allowance of 30kg.
   Their clothes weigh $15\frac{1}{2}$ kg and other items weigh 6kg 375g.
   How much more are they allowed to carry? _____

5. Aisling's mother weighs 45kg 250g and her Daddy weighs
   12kg 950g more than that.
   (a) What is Aisling's father's weight? _____
   (b) Find the total weight of both parents. _____

   Aisling weighs 31.955kg.
   (c) Aisling is _____ kg lighter than her mother.
   (d) Aisling is _____ kg lighter than her father.

# Chapter 18
## Chance

**You need:**
- coins
- dice
- red, blue, yellow and green cubes (or counters)
- non-see-through bag
- to explain outcomes and predictions

## A Looking back

1. Laura and her brother James could not agree on which TV channel to watch.

Their Dad decided that the fairest way to solve the problem was to toss a coin. Dad said that if the coin landed on heads Laura would choose and if it landed on tails James would choose.

|  | True | False |
|---|---|---|
| (a) The coin will definitely land on heads. | ☐ | ☐ |
| (b) The coin will definitely land on tails. | ☐ | ☐ |
| (c) The coin has an equal chance of landing on heads or tails. | ☐ | ☐ |

> An equal chance of something happening or not happening, is a 1 in 2 chance **or** a 50:50 chance.

2. Read the following sentences about James very carefully and then choose the best description to go with each one.

| Impossible | Poor chance | 50:50 chance | Good chance | Certain |
|---|---|---|---|---|

(a) If James tosses a coin it will land on heads._____

(b) James will be one day older in 24 hours' time._____

(c) James will never have homework to do again._____

(d) James will grow to be taller than his present height._____

(e) James will spread his wings and fly to the moon tomorrow. _____

# Possible outcomes

1. What are the possible outcomes when you toss a coin?

   _____        _____

2. Toss 2 coins and write the possible outcomes.

   _____ & _____    _____ & _____    _____ & _____

3. Look at these dice.

   (a) How many faces has a dice? _____
   (b) List the numbers shown on a dice. _____
   (c) List the possible outcomes of rolling a dice. _____
   (d) What are the chances of rolling a 6? Circle the correct answer.
       1 chance in 2, 1 chance in 4, 1 chance in 6.

4. (a) Look at the cubes in this bag. If you were told to close your
       eyes and draw out one cube, what are the possible outcomes
       in terms of the colour of the cubes?

       _____

   (b) How many colour combinations do you think are possible? _____

   (c) Now you must imagine drawing out 2 cubes.
       List all the possible colour combinations here.

       _____

       _____

   (d) Check your answers to (b) and (c) with a friend's answers.

   (e) Put 2 red, 2 yellow and 2 green cubes or counters in a
       non-see-through bag. Now draw out two cubes, replacing
       them each time before your next turn.
       Write the colour combinations here.

       _____

       _____

   (f) Did you write accurate answers to (b) and (c)? _____

# Tossing a coin

**B Moving on**

1. (a) You know that if you toss a coin, heads and tails are equally likely to occur. If you tossed a coin 50 times, what do you think the outcome would be?

Heads:_____   Tails: _____

(b) This boy tossed a coin 50 times and kept a record of the outcome.

This tally chart helped him to count the number of heads and tails. 卌 = 5

This is a frequency table showing how many times each side of the coin occurred.

| TALLY | | | FREQUENCY |
|---|---|---|---|
| 卌 卌 卌 卌 I | HEADS | | 21 |
| 卌 卌 卌 卌 卌 IIII | TAILS | | 29 |

(c) Is this the outcome you predicted in (a) above?

Yes or No? _____

2. (a) Now work with a friend and toss a coin 50 times and record the outcome here.

| TALLY CHART | | | FREQUENCY TABLE |
|---|---|---|---|
| | HEADS | | |
| | TAILS | | |

(b) Is your outcome the same as the outcome in 1(b)?
Yes or No? _____

(c) Now your friend will toss a coin 50 times.
What was the outcome?
Heads _____   Tails _____

# Rolling dice

Prediction is what you think the result will be.
Outcome is the actual result.

You know that if you roll a dice each of these six outcomes:

1   2   3   4   5   6   is equally likely to occur.

(a) What chance have you of rolling a 6?  Circle the correct answer:

1 chance in 3,  1 chance in 6,  1 chance in 8

(b) If you rolled a dice 60 times, how many times would you expect to roll a 2? _____

(c) These three children worked together to roll a dice 60 times and then recorded the outcomes like this:

| Tally Chart | | | Frequency Table |
|---|---|---|---|
| ЦНТ ЦНТ I | · | 1 | 11 |
| ЦНТ | : | 2 | 5 |
| ЦНТ ЦНТ I | ∴ | 3 | |
| ЦНТ ЦНТ ЦНТ | :: | 4 | |
| ЦНТ III | ⁙ | 5 | |
| ЦНТ ЦНТ | ⁙· | 6 | |

(d) Fill in the missing numbers on the frequency table.

(e) Is this the outcome you expected? Yes or No. _____

(f)  Which number occurred most frequently? _____

(g) Write the number of times you think each number will occur if a dice is rolled 60 times.

1 _____ 2 _____ 3 _____ 4 _____ 5 _____ 6 _____

(h) Work with 2 other children and roll a dice 60 times.

(i)  Keep a tally in your copy and draw a frequency table.

(j)  Compare your frequency table with the frequency table on this page.

(k) Compare the outcome with your predictions in (g).

# Time to experiment

Discuss these experiments with your teacher before you begin.
It would be a good idea to work in groups.
Here is what you must do for each experiment in your copy:

1.  Write down what you expect the outcome will be.

2.  Keep a tally chart.

3.  Record the results using a frequency table.

4.  Compare the results with what you expected the outcome would be.

 Don't forget to predict, record and then compare.

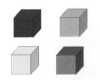

## Experiments

1.  Toss a coin 100 times. How many heads? How many tails?

2.  Roll a dice 100 times. How many times does each number on the dice occur?

3.  From a bag containing 3 cubes of one colour and 6 cubes of another colour, draw one cube 100 times.
    (Remember to replace the cube each time before you draw again.)

4.  This time put 4 cubes of one colour, 4 cubes of a second colour and 4 cubes of a third colour in the bag and draw one cube 100 times. Replace the drawn cube each time before you draw again.

**And finally!**

5.  In this experiment you roll two dice and add the two numbers.

    So if you roll  the total is 6 + 4 = 10.

    (a) Make a list of the possible totals._____

    (b) Which total do you think will be made the most? _____

    (c) Roll the pair of dice 100 times and keep a tally chart and a frequency table.

    (d) Which total occurred most often? _____

# Chapter 19
## Directed Numbers

**You need:**
- to explain BC and AD
- an atlas
- a thermometer
- to explain Fahrenheit and Celsius
- to explain 'overdrawn'
- to explain 'par' in golf

Do you know what a directed number is? Probably not. If you have any idea you can tell your teacher. But don't worry about it for the moment. I'll ask the same question again later on and by then you may have discovered the answer.

- Look at this picture of the inside of a hotel lift.
  What does O stand for?
  Yes, you're right, it stands for the Ground Floor,
  the floor that is on the same level as the
  street or road outside.
  What do 1, 2 and 3 stand for? _____

  Yes, they stand for the **first floor,** the **second floor** and the **third floor**.
  Now what does ⁻1 (negative one) stand for? _____
  What does ⁻2 (negative two) stand for? _____
  How many floors does an elevator travel from ⁺3 (positive 3) to ⁻2 (negative 2)? _____
  How many floors are there in the hotel? _____

- Now look at this thermometer.
  What does a thermometer measure? _____
  Thermometers usually show both Celsius and Fahrenheit scales.

  Fahrenheit is always used to measure your body temperature, while Celsius
  is usually used for the weather. This thermometer is in Celsius only.
  Find 0°C on the thermometer.

  When it gets very cold the liquid (mercury) in the thermometer
  goes down to 0°C. The freezing point of water is 0°C and its
  boiling point is 100°C. When it gets very cold indeed temperatures
  go below 0°C. Negative 5°C (⁻5°C) means 5 degrees below
  zero (the freezing point).

  (a) Which is warmer: 0°C or 2°C? _____ 0°C or ⁻3°C? _____

  (b) Which is colder: ⁻3°C or ⁻2°C? _____ ⁻5°C or ⁻6°C? _____

  (c) What is the difference in temperature between:
      2°C and 5°C? _____ 3°C and ⁻2°C? _____ ⁻4°C and 0°C? _____
      ⁻6°C and ⁻3°C? _____ ⁻3°C and 2°C? _____ ⁻10°C and 10°C? _____

C
— 100
— 90
— 80
— 70
— 60
— 50
— 40
— 30
— 20
— 10
— 0
— ⁻10
— ⁻20

# More directed numbers

1. Ms Cash bought a pair of shoes for €60. She had forgotten her purse and so she wrote a cheque for the €60. The shopkeeper lodged the cheque in her bank. When the time came for Ms Cash's bank to take the money from her account the bank manager discovered that she only had €50 in her account. So now her account is overdrawn. Her account is no longer in **credit**, it is now in **debit**.

   (a) How much was Ms Cash's account in credit before she bought the shoes? _____
   (b) How much is her account in debit now? _____
   (c) Can you think of a way of showing that her account is overdrawn? _____
   (d) How much does Ms Cash owe to the bank now? _____
   (e) Do you have a bank account? _____
   (f) Is your account always in credit? _____
   (g) Do you think Mum and Dad's accounts are always in credit? _____

   > '**In credit**' means you have money in the bank.
   > '**In debit**' means you owe the bank money.

   (h) By the way, what does it mean to be 'in the red'?

   _____

2. Carrauntuohill is the highest mountain peak in Ireland. It is 1041 metres **above** sea level.

   Can you name the next 2 highest mountains in Ireland and give their heights above sea level?

   _____

   _____

3. Large parts of one European country are below sea level.

   (a) Can you name the country? _____

   (b) What did the people do to solve the problem?

   _____

   _____

   (c) Have you any idea how to show in numbers that a place is 100 metres below sea level? _____

# Directed numbers again

1. Mount Juliet Golf Course in County Kilkenny is a very famous golf course. It is an 18-hole course, par 72. That means a good golfer is expected to go around the course in 72 shots.

   How would you describe the following scores?

   (a) 75 shots   <u>above par</u>   By how many shots? _____

   (b) 77 shots   _____   By how many shots? _____

   (c) 71 shots   _____   By how many shots? _____

   (d) 60 shots   _____   By how many shots? _____

   The first hole is a par four. That means that a good golfer should reach the first hole with just 4 shots. His/her score is then called a par.

   If he/she reached the hole in 3 shots he/she would have scored a <u>b</u> __ __ __ __ __.

   Describe his/her score if he/she reached the hole in 2 shots:  <u>an</u>  <u>e</u> __ __ __ __.

2. Write the next 4 numbers in these sequences.

   (a) 10, 8, 6, _____, _____, _____, _____.   (b) 13, 10, 7, _____, _____, _____, _____.

   (c) 16, 12, 8, _____, _____, _____, _____.   (d) 24, 18, 12, _____, _____, _____, _____.

   (e) 20, 15, 10, _____, _____, _____, _____.   (f) 16, 15, 13, 10, _____, _____, _____, _____.

3. Now try these.

   (a) ⁻8, ⁻6, ⁻4, _____, _____, _____, _____.   (b) ⁻15, ⁻10, ⁻5, _____, _____, _____, _____.

   (c) ⁻12, ⁻8, ⁻4, _____, _____, _____, _____.   (d) ⁻12, ⁻9, ⁻6, _____, _____, _____, _____.

   (e) ⁻100, ⁻80, ⁻60, _____, _____, _____, _____.   (f) ⁻€13, ⁻€11, ⁻€8, _____, _____, _____, _____.

4. Fill in the missing numbers.

   (a) ⁻12, ⁻11, ⁻10, _____, _____, _____, _____, _____.   (b) ⁻120, ⁻100, ⁻80, _____, _____, _____, _____.

   (c) ⁻2, 0, 2, _____, _____, _____, _____, _____.   (d) ⁻20, ⁻10, 0, _____, _____, _____, _____, _____.

   (e) ⁻75, ⁻50, ⁻25, _____, _____, _____, _____.   (f) ⁻9, ⁻6, ⁻3, _____, _____, _____, _____.

   (g) ⁻2.5, ⁻2, ⁻1.5, _____, _____, _____, _____.   (h) 2.5, 1.75, 1.25, _____, _____, _____, _____.

# Problems for you to solve

You can use your calculator to solve these problems.

1. Last Sunday the temperature in Moscow was 9°C at midday.
   By midnight it had dropped by 25°C.
   What was the temperature at midnight? _____

2. When Christmas was over Mr Cent had €2 left in his bank
   account. He bought a pair of shoes in the sale for €76.
   By how much is his account overdrawn? _____

3. This man was cleaning the hotel rooms on the third floor (⁺3).
   He forgot to bring his rubber gloves so he had to go
   down 6 floors to get them.
   On what floor were the gloves? _____

4. Jesus died in the year 32 AD but Julius Caesar, the Roman Emperor,
   died 60 years previously.
   In what year did the Emperor die? _____

5. Laura's older sister wanted to see a film which she had on video.
   The tape was stopped at 250. She had to rewind by 375 to find
   the beginning of the film.
   What was the number on the video machine
   at the beginning of the film? _____

## Did you find out?

**Did you discover what a directed number is?** _____

**Directed numbers are <u>all</u> the numbers above and below zero.**

**The set of directed numbers could be written like this:**
**(........... ⁻3, ⁻2, ⁻1, 0, 1, 2, 3...........)**

**A negative number is a number less than zero.**
**( ...........⁻6, ⁻5, ⁻4, ⁻3, ⁻2, ⁻1, 0 )**

**A positive number is a number greater than zero.**
**( 0, 1, 2, 3, 4, 5, 6 ............ )**

1. Write this improper fraction as a mixed number:

   $\frac{22}{9}$ = ___ ⬚

2. True or False? $2\frac{3}{4} > \frac{10}{4}$ _____

3. Fill in the missing mixed number on this part of the number line.

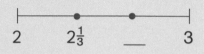

2    $2\frac{1}{3}$    ___    3

4. $2\frac{6}{8} = 2\frac{\square}{4}$

5. Markers are sold in packets of ten.

   How many packets of markers can be made from 35 markers? ___ ⬚

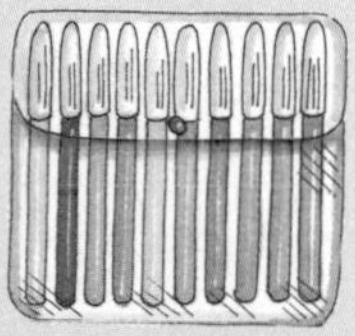

6. One CD costs €17.89. How much would 5 CDs cost? _____

7. Seán had €54.60 and he spent $\frac{1}{4}$ of it at the weekend.
   How much money had he left? _____

8. 24 x 46.375 = _____

9. 402.038 ÷ 7 = _____

10. Round this decimal to the nearest whole number: 65.709 _____

11. Would you use grammes or kilogrammes to measure
    the weight of a can of beans? _____

12. These three boys weigh 31kg 596g, 27kg 50g, and 29kg 890g.

    What is their average weight? _____

# Time to look back 4

13. Jack weighs 61kg 225g. He is 11kg 950g heavier than his mother.
    What does Jack's mother weigh? _____

14. Circle the coldest temperature:   ⁻3°C,   ⁻2°C,   0°C,   or   ⁻6°C

15. What is the difference in temperature between 2°C and ⁻4°C? _____

16. Write the next 4 numbers in this sequence: 30, 20, 10, _____, _____, _____, _____.

17. This man wrote a cheque for €90 in the supermarket
    but he had only €65 in his bank account.
    By how much is his account now overdrawn? _____

18. The car park of a hotel is two floors below ground level.
    How many floors above the car park is the fifth floor? _____

19. True or False?
    If you toss a coin there is a 50:50 chance that it will land on heads. _____

20.   What are the chances of drawing
      a yellow cube from this bag? _____

How well did you do? Tick the box that shows your score.

| ☐ | ☐ | ☐ | ☐ |
|---|---|---|---|
| 18 – 20 | 15 – 17 | 10 – 14 | 0 – 9 |
| Excellent | Very good | Good | Keep up the good work |

**You need:**
- colouring pencils
- to explain common denominator
- to revise mixed numbers, improper fraction and simplest terms

## Common denominators

$\dfrac{1}{2}$ = **numerator**

$\phantom{\dfrac{1}{2}}$ = **denominator**

Now look at these fractions: $\dfrac{6}{7}$ $\dfrac{3}{7}$ $\dfrac{5}{7}$

You will notice that the three fractions have the same denominator. We say they have a **common denominator.**

1. Write out the fractions which have **common denominators**.

(a) $\dfrac{1}{2}$, $\dfrac{4}{9}$, $\dfrac{2}{3}$, $\dfrac{5}{9}$, $\dfrac{7}{9}$ _____     (b) $\dfrac{1}{4}$, $\dfrac{5}{6}$, $\dfrac{3}{7}$, $\dfrac{5}{12}$, $\dfrac{3}{4}$ _____

(c) $\dfrac{2}{3}$, $\dfrac{7}{11}$, $\dfrac{1}{4}$, $\dfrac{5}{11}$, $\dfrac{3}{11}$ _____     (d) $\dfrac{4}{9}$, $\dfrac{1}{7}$, $\dfrac{2}{3}$, $\dfrac{5}{7}$, $\dfrac{3}{7}$ _____

2. Write four pairs of fractions which have a **common denominator**.

$\boxed{\phantom{x}}\ \boxed{\phantom{x}}$ ,   $\boxed{\phantom{x}}\ \boxed{\phantom{x}}$ ,   $\boxed{\phantom{x}}\ \boxed{\phantom{x}}$ ,   $\boxed{\phantom{x}}\ \boxed{\phantom{x}}$

Fractions which have a **common denominator** may be added.

**Example 1**

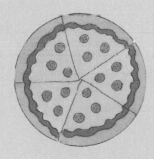

Anne ate $\dfrac{1}{5}$ of this pizza and her friend Paula ate $\dfrac{2}{5}$ of it. Colour those pieces.
What fraction of the pizza was eaten?

$\dfrac{1}{5} + \dfrac{2}{5} = \dfrac{3}{5}$     $\dfrac{3}{5}$ of the pizza was eaten.

**Common Denominator**

**Example 2**

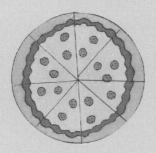

Paul ate $\dfrac{1}{8}$ of this pizza and his older brother James ate $\dfrac{3}{8}$ of it. Colour those pieces.
What fraction of the pizza was eaten?

$\dfrac{1}{8} + \dfrac{3}{8} = \dfrac{4}{8} = \dfrac{1}{2}$     $\dfrac{1}{2}$ the pizza was eaten.

**Common Denominator**

# Addition of fractions

**Example 1**

Add $\frac{5}{8}$ and $\frac{7}{8}$

$\frac{5}{8} + \frac{7}{8} = \frac{12}{8} = 1\frac{4}{8} = 1\frac{1}{2}$

1. Try these.

(a) $\frac{1}{3} + \frac{1}{3} = \boxed{\phantom{x}}$     (b) $\frac{1}{5} + \frac{3}{5} = \boxed{\phantom{x}}$     (c) $\frac{2}{7} + \frac{4}{7} = \boxed{\phantom{x}}$     (d) $\frac{5}{9} + \frac{3}{9} = \boxed{\phantom{x}}$

2. Write your answers as mixed numbers.

(a) $\frac{3}{4} + \frac{3}{4} =$ _____ (b) $\frac{5}{6} + \frac{2}{6} =$ _____ (c) $\frac{5}{8} + \frac{5}{8} =$ _____ (d) $\frac{9}{11} + \frac{4}{11} =$ ____

(e) $\frac{4}{5} + \frac{4}{5} =$ _____ (f) $\frac{6}{7} + \frac{5}{7} =$ _____ (g) $\frac{2}{3} + \frac{2}{3} =$ _____ (h) $\frac{7}{9} + \frac{5}{9} =$ ____

(i) $\frac{7}{10} + \frac{7}{10} =$ _____ (j) $\frac{7}{8} + \frac{7}{8} =$ _____ (k) $\frac{5}{6} + \frac{5}{6} =$ _____ (l) $\frac{7}{12} + \frac{7}{12} =$ ____

**Example 2**

$\frac{1}{4} + \frac{1}{2}$     $\frac{1}{2}$ is equivalent to $\frac{2}{4}$

Liam ate $\frac{1}{4}$ of this bar of chocolate and gave $\frac{1}{2}$ of the bar to his sister.

**What fraction of the bar was eaten?**

$\underset{\text{Common Denominator}}{\frac{1}{4} + \frac{2}{4}} = \frac{3}{4}$ of the bar was eaten

3. Now try these.

(a) $\frac{3}{5} + \frac{1}{10} =$ _____ (b) $\frac{3}{8} + \frac{1}{4} =$ _____ (c) $\frac{1}{2} + \frac{1}{10} =$ _____ (d) $\frac{1}{3} + \frac{5}{9} =$ _____

4. Write the answers as mixed numbers.

(a) $\frac{2}{3} + \frac{7}{9} =$ _____ (b) $\frac{3}{4} + \frac{1}{2} =$ _____ (c) $\frac{5}{6} + \frac{2}{3} =$ _____ (d) $\frac{3}{8} + \frac{3}{4} =$ _____

(e) $\frac{3}{5} + \frac{7}{10} =$ _____ (f) $\frac{7}{12} + \frac{1}{2} =$ _____ (g) $\frac{4}{5} + \frac{9}{10} =$ _____ (h) $\frac{11}{12} + \frac{3}{4} =$ _____

**Example 3**

$\frac{4}{5} + \frac{1}{2} = \frac{8}{10} + \frac{5}{10} = \frac{13}{10} = 1\frac{3}{10}$

Common Denominator

**Example 4**

$\frac{1}{2} + \frac{2}{3} = \frac{3}{6} + \frac{4}{6} = \frac{7}{6} = 1\frac{1}{6}$

Common Denominator

5. Write the answers as mixed numbers.

(a) $\frac{3}{5} + \frac{1}{2} =$ _____ (b) $\frac{3}{4} + \frac{2}{3} =$ _____ (c) $\frac{5}{6} + \frac{3}{4} =$ _____ (d) $\frac{2}{3} + \frac{5}{8} =$ ____

# Subtraction of fractions

Fractions which have a common denominator may be subtracted.

**Example 1**

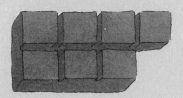

Here is $\frac{7}{8}$ of a bar of chocolate.

What fraction will be left if we take away $\frac{3}{8}$?

$\frac{7}{8} - \frac{3}{8} = \frac{4}{8}$    $\frac{4}{8} = \frac{1}{2}$    $\frac{1}{2}$ the bar will be left if $\frac{3}{8}$ is taken away

**Example 2**

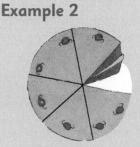

Here is $\frac{5}{6}$ of a cake. What fraction will be left if we take away $\frac{4}{6}$?

$\frac{5}{6} - \frac{4}{6} = \frac{1}{6}$    $\frac{1}{6}$ will be left if we take away $\frac{4}{6}$

1.  Now try these.

(a) $\frac{3}{4} - \frac{1}{4} =$ _____ (b) $\frac{7}{8} - \frac{5}{8} =$ _____ (c) $\frac{5}{6} - \frac{1}{6} =$ _____ (d) $\frac{7}{9} - \frac{2}{9} =$ _____

2.  (a) $\frac{7}{10} - \frac{3}{10} =$ _____ (b) $\frac{7}{12} - \frac{5}{12} =$ _____ (c) $\frac{2}{3} - \frac{1}{3} =$ _____ (d) $\frac{9}{11} - \frac{5}{11} =$ _____

**Example 3**

$\frac{3}{4} - \frac{1}{2}$    $\frac{1}{2}$ is equivalent to $\frac{2}{4}$    $\frac{3}{4} - \frac{2}{4} = \frac{1}{4}$

**Example 4**

$\frac{3}{4} - \frac{1}{3}$    $\frac{3}{4}$ is equivalent to $\frac{9}{12}$    $\frac{9}{12} - \frac{4}{12} = \frac{5}{12}$
$\frac{1}{3}$ is equivalent to $\frac{4}{12}$

3.  Now try these.

(a) $\frac{5}{8} - \frac{1}{4} =$ _____ (b) $\frac{5}{6} - \frac{1}{2} =$ _____ (c) $\frac{9}{10} - \frac{1}{5} =$ _____ (d) $\frac{3}{4} - \frac{1}{8} =$ _____

(e) $\frac{3}{4} - \frac{2}{3} =$ _____ (f) $\frac{11}{12} - \frac{1}{3} =$ _____ (g) $\frac{4}{5} - \frac{1}{2} =$ _____ (h) $\frac{7}{9} - \frac{1}{3} =$ _____

(i) $\frac{5}{6} - \frac{1}{4} =$ _____ (j) $\frac{7}{8} - \frac{1}{2} =$ _____ (k) $\frac{1}{3} - \frac{1}{9} =$ _____ (l) $\frac{2}{3} - \frac{1}{4} =$ _____

(m) $\frac{1}{3} - \frac{1}{4} =$ _____ (n) $\frac{3}{4} - \frac{1}{6} =$ _____ (o) $\frac{2}{3} - \frac{1}{2} =$ _____ (p) $\frac{1}{2} - \frac{1}{3} =$ _____

# Addition and subtraction of mixed numbers

**Example 1**

$1\frac{1}{2} + 2\frac{1}{4}$         $1\frac{2}{4}$

$=$

$1\frac{2}{4} + 2\frac{1}{4}$     $+ 2\frac{1}{4}$

Common Denominator    $3\frac{3}{4}$

**Example 2**

$2\frac{1}{2} + 2\frac{2}{3}$      $2\frac{3}{6}$   $\left(\frac{3}{6} + \frac{4}{6} = \frac{7}{6} = 1\frac{1}{6}\right)$

$=$

$2\frac{3}{6} + 2\frac{4}{6}$     $+ 2\frac{4}{{}_{1}6}$

Common Denominator    $5\frac{1}{6}$

> Now add these mixed numbers.

1. (a) $1\frac{5}{6} + 2\frac{5}{6} = $ _____ (b) $1\frac{3}{4} + 1\frac{1}{2} = $ _____ (c) $2\frac{3}{8} + \frac{3}{4} = $ _____ (d) $1\frac{5}{8} + 1\frac{1}{2} = $ _____

2. (a) $2\frac{7}{12} + 1\frac{5}{12} = $ _____ (b) $1\frac{3}{4} + 2\frac{3}{4} = $ _____ (c) $1\frac{5}{9} + 2\frac{2}{3} = $ _____ (d) $2\frac{9}{10} + 1\frac{2}{5} = $ _____

3. (a) $1\frac{5}{6} + 2\frac{5}{12} = $ _____ (b) $1\frac{4}{5} + 2\frac{1}{2} = $ _____ (c) $2\frac{2}{3} + 1\frac{5}{6} = $ _____ (d) $1\frac{7}{8} + 2\frac{3}{4} = $ _____

4. John and Mary went shopping for curtain material for their new flat. They needed $2\frac{1}{2}$ metres for one window and $4\frac{5}{6}$ metres for another window. How many metres of material did they need altogether? _____

**Example 3**

$4\frac{2}{3} - 1\frac{1}{6}$      $4\frac{4}{6}$

$=$

$4\frac{4}{6} - 1\frac{1}{6}$     $- 1\frac{1}{6}$

Common Denominator    $3\frac{3}{6} = 3\frac{1}{2}$

**Example 4**

$3\frac{1}{6} - 1\frac{3}{4} = $    $2\,3\overset{\frac{12}{12}}{\frac{2}{12}}$   $\left(\frac{12}{12} + \frac{2}{12} = \frac{14}{12}\right)$

$=$

$3\frac{2}{12} - 1\frac{9}{12}$     $- 1\frac{9}{12}$   $\left(\frac{14}{12} - \frac{9}{12} = \frac{5}{12}\right)$

Common Denominator    $1\frac{5}{12}$

> Now subtract these mixed numbers.

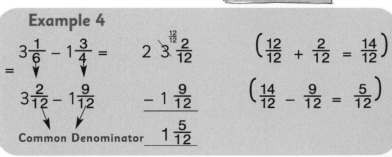

5. (a) $2\frac{3}{4} - 1\frac{1}{2} = $ _____ (b) $3\frac{5}{6} - 1\frac{2}{3} = $ _____ (c) $2\frac{7}{8} - 1\frac{1}{4} = $ _____ (d) $3\frac{7}{10} - 1\frac{1}{5} = $ _____

6. (a) $3\frac{1}{6} - 1\frac{5}{6} = $ _____ (b) $3\frac{3}{10} - 1\frac{7}{10} = $ _____ (c) $3\frac{3}{7} - 1\frac{6}{7} = $ _____ (d) $4\frac{2}{9} - 1\frac{7}{9} = $ _____

7. (a) $5\frac{1}{4} - 2\frac{5}{8} = $ _____ (b) $4\frac{1}{2} - 1\frac{3}{5} = $ _____ (c) $5\frac{1}{6} - 2\frac{3}{4} = $ _____ (d) $6\frac{1}{3} - 3\frac{3}{4} = $ _____

8. This roll of material is $8\frac{1}{4}$ metres in length. What length of material will remain on the roll if $2\frac{5}{6}$ metres is cut off and sold to a customer? _____

# Multiplying a fraction by a whole number

**Example 1**

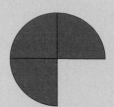 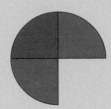 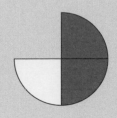

How many circles can be made from these $3 \times \frac{3}{4}$ circles?

You can see by counting the quarters:

| 4 red quarters | 4 green quarters | and | 1 yellow quarter |

↓ ↓ ↓

| 1 full circle | 1 full circle | and | 1 quarter = $2\frac{1}{4}$ |

Before multiplying a fraction by a whole number you must write the whole number as an improper fraction like this:

$3 = \frac{3}{1}$   $4 = \frac{4}{1}$   $6 = \frac{6}{1}$   $5 = \frac{5}{1}$   $9 = \frac{9}{1}$

Now let us see how many circles can be made from the $3 \times \frac{3}{4}$ circles by multiplying.

1. Change the whole number into an improper fraction: $3 = \frac{3}{1}$

2. Multiply the numerators ⟶ $3 \times 3 = 9$
3. Multiply the denominators ⟶ $1 \times 4 = 4$   $= 2\frac{1}{4}$

**Example 2**

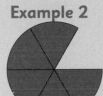  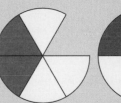

How many circles can be made from these $4 \times \frac{5}{6}$ circles?

By counting the sixths:

   1 red circle, 1 green circle, 1 yellow circle and 2 pink sixths = $3\frac{2}{6} = 3\frac{1}{3}$

By multiplying: $4 \times \frac{5}{6}$

1. Change 4 to an improper fraction. $4 = \frac{4}{1}$
2. Multiply the numerators ⟶ $4 \times 5 = 20$
3. Multiply the denominators ⟶ $1 \times 6 = 6$   $= 3\frac{2}{6} = 3\frac{1}{3}$

# Multiplying again

1. Try this question:

Six children had $\frac{2}{3}$ of a pizza each. How much pizza did they eat between them?   $6 \times \frac{2}{3}$

(a) Change the whole number to an improper fraction.

(b) Multiply the numerators ➡  ___ x ___ = 

(c) Multiply the denominators ➡  ___ x ___ = _____ = 

Now find the answers to the following questions.

2. (a) $9 \times \frac{1}{2}$ = _____    (b) $8 \times \frac{1}{6}$ = _____    (c) $9 \times \frac{2}{5}$ = _____    (d) $7 \times \frac{2}{3}$ = _____

3. (a) $4 \times \frac{3}{8}$ = _____    (b) $2 \times \frac{3}{4}$ = _____    (c) $5 \times \frac{2}{7}$ = _____    (d) $3 \times \frac{5}{8}$ = _____

4. (a) $5 \times \frac{5}{9}$ = _____    (b) $7 \times \frac{3}{10}$ = _____    (c) $3 \times \frac{7}{11}$ = _____    (d) $4 \times \frac{5}{12}$ = _____

5. (a) $6 \times \frac{4}{6}$ = _____    (b) $8 \times \frac{7}{8}$ = _____    (c) $6 \times \frac{7}{9}$ = _____    (d) $9 \times \frac{7}{8}$ = _____

## Problems for you to solve

1. A teacher was explaining the meaning of halves to a group of eight children. She gave half an orange to each of the children.

How many oranges did she use? ▭ x / x ▭ = _____ oranges

2. Four boys ate $\frac{3}{4}$ of a bar of chocolate each after school.

How many bars of chocolates did they eat altogether? ▭ x / x ▭ = _____ bars

3. (a) Each of these small cartons of milk contains 250ml.

   What fraction of a litre does each carton contain? ▭

   (b) Nine children from fifth class drank a carton of milk each at lunchtime.

   How many litres of milk did they drink? ▭ x / x ▭ = _____ litres

# More problems for you to solve

1. This jug holds 1 litre of orange juice and each glass can hold $\frac{1}{8}$ of a litre. Tom had 2 glasses of juice and his older brother had 3 glasses.

    (a) What fraction of the litre did they drink between them?

    (b) What fraction of the juice remained?

    (c) How many millilitres of juice did they drink? _____

2. Louise and Julie shared some of Tom's thirty colouring pencils during maths class. Tom took $\frac{1}{5}$, Julie took $\frac{1}{6}$ and Louise took $\frac{1}{3}$ of the pencils.

    (a) How many pencils did each child take? _____ _____ _____

    (b) What fraction of the pencils did the children use?

    (b) How many pencils were not used? _____

3. Tom's friend, Paul, was in charge of distributing the cartons of milk at lunchtime. He distributed $\frac{7}{8}$ of the 32 cartons which were delivered to the classroom. How many cartons of milk were left over? _____

4. Tom's father bought three pizzas of equal size for dinner. The family ate the following amounts of a pizza each:

    Tom's mother: $\frac{3}{4}$    Tom: $\frac{3}{4}$    Maria: $\frac{1}{2}$    Tom's father: $\frac{2}{3}$

    (Write your answers as mixed numbers.)

    (a) How much pizza did Tom and his father eat between them? _____

    (b) How much altogether did Maria and her mother eat? _____

    (c) How much pizza was eaten altogether? _____

    (d) How much pizza was left over? _____

5. After dinner Tom went to the shop. He spent $\frac{1}{8}$ of his money on a bar of chocolate and $\frac{1}{4}$ of his money on a drink.

    (a) How much was the drink? _____

    (b) What fraction of his money did Tom spend?

    (c) How much money had he left? _____

# Go for it!

1.  Write these improper fractions as mixed numbers.

    (a) $\frac{14}{10}$ _____   (b) $\frac{23}{3}$ = _____   (c) $\frac{26}{12}$ = _____   (d) $\frac{30}{9}$ = _____

    (e) $\frac{35}{10}$ = _____   (f) $\frac{21}{6}$ = _____   (g) $\frac{44}{8}$ = _____   (h) $\frac{36}{5}$ = _____

2.  Write these mixed numbers as improper fractions.

    (a) $3\frac{3}{4}$ = _____   (b) $2\frac{7}{8}$ = _____   (c) $3\frac{4}{5}$ = _____   (d) $4\frac{9}{10}$ = _____

    (e) $6\frac{5}{6}$ = _____   (f) $7\frac{8}{9}$ = _____   (g) $4\frac{5}{7}$ = _____   (h) $8\frac{7}{8}$ = _____

3.  Put the correct sign, **>**, **=** or **<** between these pairs.

    (a) $2\frac{7}{12}$  $2\frac{3}{4}$   (b) $5\frac{5}{9}$  $5\frac{2}{3}$   (c) $3\frac{9}{12}$  $3\frac{3}{4}$   (d) $2\frac{1}{2}$  $2\frac{7}{10}$

    (e) $\frac{16}{10}$  $\frac{8}{5}$   (f) $\frac{9}{2}$  $\frac{29}{6}$   (g) $\frac{37}{8}$  $\frac{19}{4}$   (h) $\frac{40}{12}$  $\frac{11}{3}$

    (i) $2\frac{1}{6}$  $\frac{35}{12}$   (j) $3\frac{1}{3}$  $\frac{14}{4}$   (k) $\frac{11}{2}$  $\frac{20}{3}$   (l) $\frac{15}{4}$  $3\frac{7}{8}$

4.  Write the answers as mixed numbers.

    (a) $\frac{5}{9} + \frac{7}{9}$ = _____   (b) $\frac{3}{4} + \frac{3}{4}$ = _____   (c) $\frac{7}{8} + \frac{3}{4}$ = _____   (d) $\frac{7}{12} + \frac{11}{12}$ = _____

5.  (a) $6\frac{2}{3} + 5\frac{2}{3}$ = _____   (b) $3\frac{7}{9} + 2\frac{2}{3}$ = _____   (c) $3\frac{11}{12} + 4\frac{2}{3}$ = _____   (d) $1\frac{9}{10} + 3\frac{1}{2}$ = _____

6.  (a) $\frac{8}{9} - \frac{1}{3}$ = _____   (b) $\frac{5}{6} - \frac{2}{3}$ = _____   (c) $\frac{11}{12} - \frac{1}{2}$ = _____   (d) $\frac{3}{4} - \frac{7}{12}$ = _____

7.  (a) $3\frac{7}{8} - 1\frac{1}{2}$ = _____   (b) $6\frac{5}{12} - 4\frac{3}{4}$ = _____   (c) $7\frac{1}{2} - 3\frac{9}{10}$ = _____   (d) $5\frac{1}{9} - 1\frac{2}{3}$ = _____

8.  Find the perimeter of this shape.

    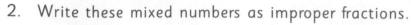

    $5\frac{1}{6}$ m

    6 m

    $2\frac{3}{4}$ m

    $10\frac{7}{12}$ m

    Perimeter: _____ m

9.  What is the perimeter of a square if the sides are $3\frac{1}{3}$ metres in length? _____

# Chapter 22

### Time

**You need:**
- a calendar
- to explain a.m. and p.m.
- to explain the 24-hour clock
- a 24-hour clock

## A Looking back

1. (a) How many minutes in an hour? _____

   (b) How many hours in a day? _____

   (c) How many days in a week? _____

   (d) How many weeks in a year? _____

   (e) How many days in a non-leap year? _____

   (f) How many years in a decade? _____

   (g) How many years in a century? _____

   (h) How many months, weeks or days to your birthday? _____

   (i) In what year were you born? _____

   (j) In what year will you celebrate your twenty-first birthday? _____

   (k) Change 183 minutes to hours and minutes. _____ hrs _____ mins

   (l) Change 2 hours 55 mins to minutes. _____ mins

   (m) Show twenty minutes past seven on both of these clocks.

 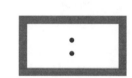

2. What time was it 15 minutes before these times?

   (a) `4:05` | : |   (b) `12:35` | : |   (c) `7:10` | : |   (d) `3:30` | : |

3. Draw hands on these clock faces to show what time it will be 35 minutes later than the digital times shown.

   (a) `12:36`      (b) `2:29`

4. Liam leaves home for school at 8.25 and arrives home at 2.55.

   How many hours and minutes is he away from home? _____ hrs _____ mins

5. Liam's school was built in 1984. How many years ago is that? _____

6. Liam's mother works from 9.00 to 4.00, five days a week.

   How many hours does she work in a week? _____

# Class timetables

Here is part of a fifth class timetable.

|  | Monday | Tuesday | Wednesday | Thursday | Friday |
|---|---|---|---|---|---|
| 9.00 – 9.50 | English | Gaeilge | English | Gaeilge | English |
| 9.50 – 10.45 | Maths | Maths | Gaeilge | Maths | Maths |
| 10.45 – 11.00 | SOS | SOS | SOS | SOS | SOS |
| 11.00 – 11.55 | Gaeilge | History | Geography | Science | Music |
| 11.55 – 12.35 | PE | English | Library Time | English | PE |

Now answer these questions.

1. How many minutes long is:
   (a) the first lesson? _____mins
   (b) the second lesson? _____mins
   (c) the third lesson? _____mins
   (d) the fourth lesson? _____mins

2. How many hours and minutes are spent on the following subjects per week?
   (a) English: _____hrs _____mins
   (b) Gaeilge: _____hrs _____mins
   (c) Mathematics: _____hrs _____mins

3. How much longer per week is spent on:
   (a) English than Maths? _____hrs _____mins
   (b) Maths than Gaeilge? _____hrs _____mins

4. The pupils have a half-hour lunch break from 12.35 to 1.05, in addition to their morning break. How much free time do the pupils have
   (a) per day? _____mins
   (b) per week? _____hrs _____mins

5. The pupils spend _____ mins longer on Physical Education than on Music per week.

# Cinema timetable

This timetable shows the daily screening times of the current films at the Star six screen cinema.

| White Knight | 2.25, | 4.40, | 6.55, | 9.20 |
|---|---|---|---|---|
| Fear! | 3.00, | 5.10, | 7.20, | 9.30 |
| Time Traveller | 1.10, | 3.40, | 6.20, | 9.00 |
| Spider People | 1.40, | 4.20, | 7.00, | 9.40 |
| Kool Kids | 2.15, | 4.40, | 6.50, | 9.15 |
| Wind Walkers | 1.15, | 3.55, | 6.35, | 9.15 |

Now answer these questions.

1. The second screening of **White Knight** starts at _____.
2. The last screening of **Wind Walkers** starts at _____.
3. It takes John 25 minutes to walk to the cinema. At what time should he leave home to arrive at the cinema ten minutes before the third screening of **Spider People**? _____
4. The cinema opens half an hour before the screening of the earliest film. At what time does the cinema open? _____
5. The cinema closes at midnight. The cinema is open for _____ hrs _____ mins per day.

## a.m. and p.m.

Read this paragraph.

While Paul's mother was out with friends on Monday afternoon, her sister Anne phoned from England to say that she was coming to visit on the following Saturday. Paul took the call and here is the message he wrote for his mother.

'Auntie Anne arriving Dublin Airport next Saturday at half past ten.'

Paul's mother was delighted that her sister was coming but she needed more information regarding the time of arrival.

Was Anne arriving at 10.30 in the morning or 10.30 at night? To avoid such confusion we use a.m. and p.m.

**a.m.** is short for **ante meridian** – Latin words meaning 'before midday'.

**p.m.** is short for **post meridian** – Latin words meaning 'after midday'.

For all times between midnight and midday we use a.m.

For all times between midday and midnight we use p.m.

For example, we come to school at about 9.00 a.m. and go home at about 2.30 p.m.

# Moving on – a.m. and p.m.

1. Look at this clock. It shows the 24 hours in a day.
   Fill in the missing a.m. and p.m. times.

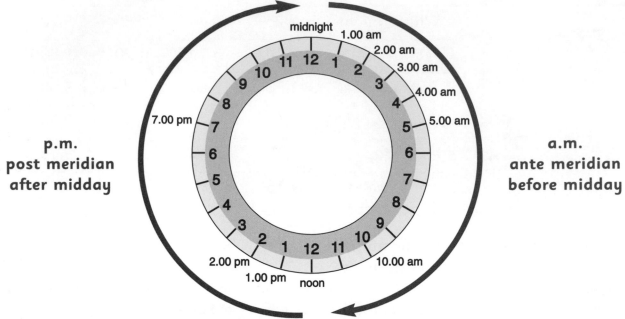

**p.m.**
**post meridian**
**after midday**

midnight
1.00 am
2.00 am
3.00 am
4.00 am
5.00 am
7.00 pm
2.00 pm
1.00 pm
noon
10.00 am

**a.m.**
**ante meridian**
**before midday**

2. Write these times using a.m. or p.m.

   (a) 8 o'clock in the morning _____ .   (b) $\frac{1}{4}$ hour before noon _____ .

   (c) 4.30 in the afternoon _____ .   (d) $\frac{1}{2}$ hour before midnight _____ .

   (e) 1 hour after midnight _____ .   (f) 7 o'clock in the evening _____ .

   (g) $\frac{1}{4}$ past 3 in the afternoon _____ .   (h) ten to nine at night _____ .

3. How many hours are there between these times?

   (a) 8.00 a.m. and 1.00 p.m. _____ .   (b) noon and 11.00 p.m. _____ .

   (c) midnight and 7.00 a.m. _____ .   (d) 3.00 p.m. and 3.00 a.m. _____ .

   (e) 8.00 p.m. and 2.00 a.m. _____ .   (f) 1.00 a.m. and 2.00 p.m. _____ .

4. Paul's aunt was arriving at the airport at 10.30 a.m.

   (a) Mark that time in red on the above clock face.

   Write the answers to Questions (b) and (c) using a.m. or p.m.

   (b) At what time should the family leave home if the journey to
       the airport takes $1\frac{1}{2}$ hours? _____ .

   (c) At what time would the family arrive home if they left
       the airport at 11.15 a.m.? _____ .

   (d) How many hours and minutes were the family away from home?

       _____hrs _____mins

# The 24-hour clock

Look at the diagram on the left-hand side of this page. It shows one day, 24 hours from midnight to midnight in the life of an eleven-year-old child.

| | |
|---|---|
| Midnight __ | Sleeping |
| 1.00 a.m.__ | |
| 2.00 a.m.__ | |
| 3.00 a.m.__ | |
| 4.00 a.m.__ | |
| 5.00 a.m.__ | |
| 6.00 a.m.__ | |
| 7.00 a.m.__ | |
| 8.00 a.m.__ | Showering Having breakfast |
| 9.00 a.m.__ | Going to school |
| 10.00 a.m__ | In school |
| 11.00 a.m__ | |
| Midday or Noon __ | |
| 1.00 p.m.__ | |
| 2.00 p.m.__ | |
| 3.00 p.m.__ | |
| 4.00 p.m.__ | Journey home Having a snack |
| 5.00 p.m.__ | Homework |
| 6.00 p.m.__ | Outside playing |
| 7.00 p.m.__ | Having dinner |
| 8.00 p.m.__ | Homework Watching TV with family |
| 9.00 p.m.__ | Reading |
| 10.00 p.m__ | Getting ready for bed |
| 11.00 p.m__ | Sleeping |
| Midnight __ | |

Notice that the times before noon are marked a.m. and the times after noon are marked p.m.

1. Write what the child might have been doing or where she was at the following times.
   (a) 1.05 a.m.  _____
   (b) 8.30 a.m.  _____
   (c) midday  _____
   (d) 3.30 p.m.  _____
   (e) 4.45 p.m.  _____
   (f) 6.15 p.m.  _____
   (g) 8.30 p.m.  _____
   (h) 11.30 p.m.  _____

2. Write these times using a.m. or p.m.
   (a) 11.45 in the morning  _____
   (b) 11.30 at night  _____
   (c) 6.30 in the evening  _____
   (d) 3.22 in the afternoon  _____
   (e) 2.00 in the morning.  _____

3. Look at the diagram on the right-hand side of this page. This time the 24 hours of one day are shown in a.m. and p.m. time **and** in 24-hour clock time.
   We do not need a.m. and p.m. in the 24-hour clock. 8.00 a.m. is written 08.00 and 8.00 p.m. is written 20.00.

   You always use 4 digits when writing 24-hour clock times.
   7.02 a.m. = 07.02
   7.02 p.m. = 19.02

| | |
|---|---|
| Midnight __ | 00.00 |
| 1.00 a.m.__ | 01.00 |
| 2.00 a.m.__ | 02.00 |
| 3.00 a.m.__ | 03.00 |
| 4.00 a.m.__ | 04.00 |
| 5.00 a.m.__ | 05.00 |
| 6.00 a.m.__ | 06.00 |
| 7.00 a.m.__ | 07.00 |
| 8.00 a.m.__ | 08.00 |
| 9.00 a.m.__ | 09.00 |
| 10.00 a.m__ | 10.00 |
| 11.00 a.m__ | 11.00 |
| Midday or Noon __ | 12.00 |
| 1.00 p.m.__ | 13.00 |
| 2.00 p.m.__ | 14.00 |
| 3.00 p.m.__ | 15.00 |
| 4.00 p.m.__ | 16.00 |
| 5.00 p.m.__ | 17.00 |
| 6.00 p.m.__ | 18.00 |
| 7.00 p.m.__ | 19.00 |
| 8.00 p.m.__ | 20.00 |
| 9.00 p.m.__ | 21.00 |
| 10.00 p.m__ | 22.00 |
| 11.00 p.m__ | 23.00 |
| Midnight __ | 00.00 |

# a.m. and p.m. and 24-hour time

1. Write these times using the 24 hour clock.
   (a) 7.04 a.m. _____   (b) 11.30 p.m. _____   (c) 12.15 p.m. _____
   (d) 8.45 a.m. _____   (e) midday _____   (f) midnight _____

2. Write these 24 hour clock times using a.m. or p.m.
   (a) 18.30 _____   (b) 07.15 _____   (c) 13.00 _____
   (d) 00.00 _____   (e) 20.50 _____   (f) 05.30 _____

3. Fill in the times using (a) a.m. or p.m. and (b) 24 hour clock times.
   (a) I get up at                                _____   _____
   (b) School starts at                          _____   _____
   (c) I have lunch at                           _____   _____
   (d) School finishes at                        _____   _____
   (e) I arrive home from school at              _____   _____
   (f) I have dinner at                          _____   _____
   (g) My favourite TV programme starts at       _____   _____
   (h) My favourite TV programme finishes at     _____   _____
   (i) I go to bed at                            _____   _____
   (j) I am usually asleep by                    _____   _____

4. (a) Tom's father watched two sports programmes on television on Saturday,
      from 3.10 p.m. to 4.55 p.m. and from 7.00 p.m. to 7.55 p.m.
      How many hours and minutes was he watching TV? _____hrs _____mins

   (b) Tom watched TV from 7.05 p.m. until 8.55 p.m.
      How many hours and minutes did Tom spend watching TV?

      _____hrs _____mins

   (c) For how much longer was Tom's father watching TV than Tom? _____

   (d) Tom's parents went to the supermarket at 11.30 and returned at 13.50.
      How many hours and minutes were they out of the house? _____hrs _____mins

   (e) Tom's older brother went to town with friends at 14.15. They came home
      2 hours 30 minutes later. At what time did they return? _____

   (f) Tom's father went to bed at 00.55. Tom went to bed 1 hour and 45 minutes
      before his dad. At what time did Tom go to bed? _____

   (g) Tom woke up 7hrs 55mins after he went to bed.
      At what time did Tom wake up? _____a.m.

# More timetables

This timetable shows the departure times and arrival times of six flights out of Dublin.

1. Write the length of each flight in hours and minutes.

| Depart Dublin | Arrival Times | | Length of Flight |
|---|---|---|---|
| 7.00 a.m. | London | 8.35 a.m. | |
| 11.00 a.m. | Rome | 3.05 p.m. | |
| 11.30 a.m. | New York | 4.25 p.m. | |
| 4.00 p.m. | Cork | 4.50 p.m. | |
| 7.00 p.m. | Los Angeles | 5.15 a.m. | |
| 11.00 p.m. | Barcelona | 2.20 a.m. | |

2. Which was the longest flight? Dublin to _____

3. Which was the shortest flight? Dublin to _____

4. What is the difference in hours and minutes between the longest and shortest flight? _____hrs _____mins

5. How many hours and minutes longer is the flight to Rome than the flight to London? _____hrs _____mins

6. Calculate the length of time it would take for a return flight from Dublin to each of these 6 cities.

   (a) London _____   (b) Rome _____   (c) New York _____

   (d) Cork _____   (e) Los Angeles _____   (f) Barcelona _____

7. Write out the timetable in your copy using 24-hour time.

8. This table shows the times of high tide, morning and evening for Dublin and for four other places one day in September.
   It shows that high tides in Bray, for example, are 6 minutes earlier than in Dublin.
   Calculate the high tide times for **Bray**, **Skerries**, **Wicklow** and **Wexford Harbour**.

| Dublin | 12.30 | 00.36 | |
|---|---|---|---|
| Bray | _____ | _____ | (⁻6 mins) |
| Skerries | _____ | _____ | (⁻16 mins) |
| Wicklow | _____ | _____ | (⁻41 mins) |
| Wexford Harbour | _____ | _____ | (⁻5 hrs 35 mins) |

**You need:**
– graduated measuring jugs
– calculators
– 6 items for Question 1, p.142
– to explain 'pasteurise'

Do you still remember what capacity means?
It means the amount of liquid that a container can hold.

> Capacity is measured in litres and millilitres.
> There are 1000 millilitres in 1 litre or 1000ml = 1l.

The capacity of this carton is 1 litre.
It can hold 1 litre of milk.

The capacity of this spoon is about 5ml.
The spoon holds about 5ml of medicine.

1.  Now let's look to see what kind of containers are in the classroom.

    (a) Make a list of 5 of those containers.

    (i) _____, (ii) _____, (iii) _____, (iv) _____, (v) _____

    (b) Now what about the containers that the children in your class are using for their lunch drink? **Make a list of the different types of containers we can drink from.** _____

    _____

    (c) Sometimes the capacity of the container is written on the label but if not, or if the label is missing, can you find the capacity of 4 of the containers with the help of the classroom measuring jug?

    (i) _____, (ii) _____, (iii) _____, (iv) _____.

2.  Make a list of 5 containers that hold more than 1 litre.

    _____

3.  Make a list of 5 containers that hold less than 1 litre.

    _____

# Litres and millilitres

1. Would you use litres or millilitres to measure the following items?
Tick the correct one.

| | Item | l | ml |
|---|---|---|---|
| 1 | Petrol | | |
| 2 | Cough bottle | | |
| 3 | Washing-up liquid | | |
| 4 | Shampoo | | |
| 5 | Sauce | | |
| 6 | Nail varnish | | |
| 7 | Heating oil | | |
| 8 | Milk at the creamery | | |

2. Write as litres and millilitres in two ways.

(a) 1370ml     =     1l 370ml     =     1.370l

(b) 2450ml     =     _____     =     _____

(c) 5000ml     =     _____     =     _____

(d) 9005ml     =     _____     =     _____

(e) 8090ml     =     _____     =     _____

3. Do you remember from fourth class how to add, subtract, multiply and divide
using litres and millilitres?
These four examples will help you as you work your way through the rest of this chapter.

---

**Example 1**     6l 290ml + 2l 860ml

```
  6l  290ml              6.290l
+ 2l  860ml    or      + 2.860l
  9l  150ml              9.150l
```

---

**Example 2**     3l 750ml – 1l 895ml

```
  3l  750ml              3.750l
– 1l  895ml    or      – 1.895l
  1l  855ml              1.855l
```

---

**Example 3**     3l 275 ml x 4

```
  3l  275ml              3.275l
      x 4      or            x 4
 13l 100ml              13.100l
```

---

**Example 4**     12l 560ml ÷ 8

```
8 12l 560ml            8 12.560l
  1l 570ml    or          1.570l
```

---

# Estimate and measure

1. Your teacher will find the 6 items listed in the table below.
   Estimate their capacity in millilitres to the nearest 100ml and write it in the table below.
   Then, if the capacity is not written on the label, you can find the exact capacity by using the measuring jug.

| | Item | Estimate | Exact Capacity | Difference |
|---|---|---|---|---|
| 1 | Carton of fruit drink | | | |
| 2 | Bottle of water | | | |
| 3 | Cup | | | |
| 4 | Mug | | | |
| 5 | Kettle | | | |
| 6 | Bucket | | | |

How accurate was your estimate?    Good ☐    Very Good ☐    Excellent ☐

2. List the containers in order of size starting with the container with the least capacity.

_____

3. Now with your calculator, you can find out the **total** exact capacity of the 6 items in the table above. Then find the total difference between your estimate and the exact capacity.

   Total estimated capacity: _____

   Total exact capacity:      _____

   Difference:                _____

   To show 3l 295ml on a calculator key in 3.295

4. Now find the average capacity of the 6 items by dividing the total capacity by 6. _____

   Check your answer using a calculator.

**To find out:**
5. At home find the container that you think has (a) the largest capacity  (b) the smallest capacity and estimate the capacity of each one.
   Estimated capacity          (a) _____ (b) _____
   Then find the exact capacity  (a) _____ (b) _____

# Problems for you to solve

1. Find the cost of 18 litres of petrol at 90c per litre. _____

2. Paul's fish tank holds 12 litres of water. He changes the water once a week and fills it up with a jug that holds 250ml. How many jugfuls will it take to fill the tank? _____

3. When Sinéad had a cough her Mammy bought her a cough bottle in the chemist shop. The bottle contained 200ml of the mixture. She was told to take one 5ml spoonful of it twice a day. How many days would the bottle last? _____

4. From a $2\frac{1}{2}$ litre orange bottle Michelle drank 650ml. How much orange was left in the bottle? _____

5. If a family uses 2 litres of milk a day what would be the cost of milk for the month of July at 95c per litre? _____ (Check your calendar for the number of days in July.)

6. The pupils in Scoil Cholmcille are provided with cartons of milk like this one every day. The fifth class pupils used 26 cartons last Monday. How many litres and millilitres is that? _____ l _____ ml

7. This carton holds 330ml of fruit juice. How much juice is needed to fill 9 cartons? _____

8. The petrol tank in Mr Ford's car holds 42 litres of petrol. The car goes for 25 kilometres per litre of petrol. How many kilometres can it go on a full tank of petrol? _____

# Welcome to Greenvale Dairy

There are 18 dairy farmers in the Greenvale area and they send their milk to Greenvale Dairy. Some farmers put the milk in creamery cans and bring it to the dairy with their tractor. The milk tanker comes to the other farmers to bring their milk to the dairy. A creamery can holds 30 litres while a tanker can carry 5000 litres.

Answer the following questions.

1. (a) Farmer O'Brien brings 3 cans a day to the dairy.

    How many litres does he bring in a week? _____

    (b) He is paid 20c a litre.

    How much will be in his weekly cheque from the dairy? _____

2. How much does the dairy pay for a full tanker of milk? _____

3. Farmer Murphy is the biggest supplier of milk. He supplies 850 litres of milk per day.

    (a) How many litres does he supply in a full week? _____

    (b) How many litres does he supply in the month of July? _____

    (c) How much will be in his weekly cheque from the dairy? _____

    (d) How much will he get for the month of July? _____

4. The dairy takes in 12,600 litres of milk per day.

    What is the average amount of milk produced by each farmer every day? _____

5. The dairy pasteurises the milk, puts it into 1 litre cartons and sells it in the town at 90c a litre.

    (a) How much money does the dairy take in every week? _____

    (b) If the dairy pays out €37 250 in wages and costs each week, how much profit does it make? _____

**You need:**
- a calculator
- colouring pencils

The symbol **%** stands for 'per cent'.
It comes from Latin and it means 'per hundred'.

45

35

20

100 children in fifth class were asked which of these foods did they prefer.

- 45 out of the 100 chose pizza. That can be written in 3 ways: $\frac{45}{100}$ or 0.45 or **45%.**

- 35 out of the 100 chose burgers. That can be written as $\frac{35}{100}$ or 0.35 or **35%**.

- 20 chose chicken. That can be written as $\frac{20}{100}$ or 0.20 or **20%**.

1. What percentage of these 100 squares is coloured?

(a)

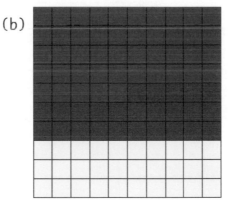

(b)

(c)

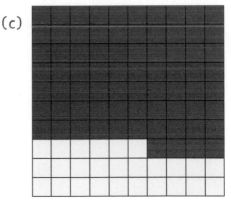

Red _____ %

Blue _____ %

Yellow _____ %

Red & Yellow _____ %

Red _____ %

Blue _____ %

Yellow _____ %

Red & Blue _____ %

Red _____ %

Blue _____ %

Yellow _____ %

Blue & Yellow _____ %

# Inisbeg Youth Club survey

1. There are 100 members in Inisbeg Youth Club and they were asked which of these indoor games they preferred.

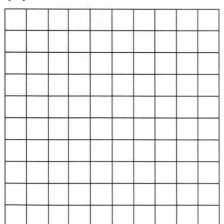 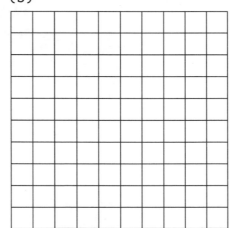 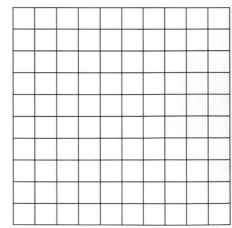

**36**        **24**        **40**

Can you fill the gaps?

_____ out of the 100 chose chess. That can be written in 3 ways: $\frac{}{100}$ or 0. _____ or _____

The symbol _____ stands for per _ _ _ _ . It means per h _ _ _ _ _ _ _ .

_____ out of the 100 chose draughts. That can be written as $\frac{}{100}$ or 0._____ or _____.

_____ chose table tennis. That can be written as $\frac{}{100}$ or _____ or _____.

2. Colour in these squares as shown below.

(a)

(b)

(c)

| 25% blue | 45% black | 70% orange |
| 40% red | 30% green | 25% blue |
| 35% yellow | 25% blue | – remainder green |

146

# What percentage?

1. What percentage of each shape is coloured?

(a)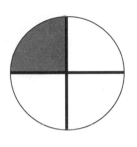

_____

(b)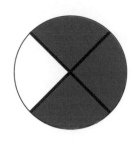

_____

(c)

_____

(d) _____

(e) _____

(f) _____

2. What percentage of each set is circled?

(a)

(b)

(c)

_____

_____

_____

(d)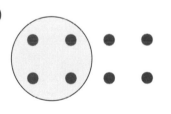

(e)

(f)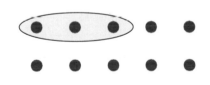

_____

_____

_____

3. What percentage is:

(a) $\frac{1}{2}$ _____    (b) $\frac{1}{4}$ _____    (c) $\frac{1}{5}$ _____    (d) $\frac{3}{4}$ _____

(e) $\frac{1}{10}$ _____    (f) $\frac{2}{5}$ _____    (g) $\frac{3}{10}$ _____    (h) $\frac{3}{5}$ _____

(i) $\frac{4}{5}$ _____    (j) $\frac{7}{10}$ _____    (k) $\frac{9}{10}$ _____    (l) $\frac{1}{8}$ _____

# Fractions, decimals, percentages

1. Change these percentages to fractions.

(a) 50% = $\boxed{\phantom{-}}$    (b) 25% = $\boxed{\phantom{-}}$    (c) 75% = $\boxed{\phantom{-}}$    (d) 20% = $\boxed{\phantom{-}}$

(e) 10% = $\boxed{\phantom{-}}$    (f) 30% = $\boxed{\phantom{-}}$    (g) 40% = $\boxed{\phantom{-}}$    (h) 60% = $\boxed{\phantom{-}}$

(i) 80% = $\boxed{\phantom{-}}$    (j) 90% = $\boxed{\phantom{-}}$    (k) 70% = $\boxed{\phantom{-}}$    (l) 45% = $\boxed{\phantom{-}}$

2. Change these percentages to decimals.

(a) 30% = 0._____    (b) 60% = _____    (c) 25% = _____    (d) 75% = _____

(e) 10% = _____    (f) 20% = _____    (g) 48% = _____    (h) 90% = _____

(i) 15% = _____    (j) 35% = _____    (k) 45% = _____    (l) 95% = _____

3. Change these decimals to percentages and then to fractions. The first one is done for you.

(a) 0.75 = 75% = $\frac{75}{100}$ = $\frac{3}{4}$    (b) 0.25 = _____ = _____ = _____

(c) 0.45 = _____ = _____ = _____    (d) 0.36 = _____ = _____ = _____

(e) 0.5 = _____ = _____ = _____    (f) 0.1 = _____ = _____

(g) 0.2 = _____ = _____ = _____    (h) 0.9 = _____ = _____

4. Change these fractions to percentages and then to decimals. The first one is done for you.

(a) $\frac{1}{4}$ = 25% = 0.25    (b) $\frac{3}{4}$ = _____ = _____    (c) $\frac{1}{5}$ = _____ = _____

(d) $\frac{1}{10}$ = _____ = _____    (e) $\frac{3}{10}$ = _____ = _____    (f) $\frac{2}{5}$ = _____ = _____

(g) $\frac{7}{10}$ = _____ = _____    (h) $\frac{3}{5}$ = _____ = _____    (i) $\frac{4}{5}$ = _____ = _____

(j) $\frac{9}{10}$ = _____ = _____    (k) $\frac{10}{10}$ = _____ = _____    (l) $\frac{1}{20}$ = _____ = _____

# Finding percentages

**Example 1**
Find 50% of €20.

$50\% = \frac{50}{100} = \frac{1}{2}$

$\frac{1}{2}$ of €20 = €10

Ans: €10

**Example 2**
Find 10% of 80.

$10\% = \frac{10}{100} = \frac{1}{10}$

$\frac{1}{10}$ of 80 = 8

Ans: 8

1. Complete the following:

   (a) 50% of 24 sweets = _____ sweets

   (b) 25% of 36 marbles = _____ marbles

   (c) 20% of €10 = €_____

   (d) 10% of 80 boys = _____ boys

   (e) 40% of 20 girls = _____ girls

   (f) 75% of 40 chairs = _____ chairs

   (g) 60% of 15 teachers = _____ teachers

   (h) 90% of 200 soldiers = _____ soldiers

   (i) 20% of €120 = €_____

   (j) 30% of 240 pupils = _____ pupils

2. Complete the following:

   (a) 50% of 1 metre     = _____

   (b) 25% of 1 kg       = _____

   (c) 10% of 1 km       = _____

   (d) 20% of 1 litre    = _____

   (e) 40% of 10 metres  = _____

   (f) 10% of 2 km       = _____

   (g) 50% of 5 litres   = _____

   (h) 75% of 1 km       = _____

   (i) 25% of 6 kg       = _____

   (j) 20% of 2 m        = _____

3. Now try these. Write the letters from the beginning of each word.
   The first one is done for you.

   (a) 50% of FAMOUS is **FAM**

   (b) 25% of HAND is _____

   (c) 20% of TRAIN is _____

   (d) 75% of DOGS is _____

   (e) 40% of SUGAR is _____

   (f) 10% of CLASSROOMS is _____

   (g) 60% of FINGERNAIL is _____

   (h) 80% of SILLY is _____

# Problems for you to solve

1. Michael had €20 in his money box. He spent 25% of it on a birthday present for his friend James. How much had he left? _____

2. There were 20 boxes of sweets in this pile.
   (a) How many are left? _____

   (b) What fraction is gone? _____

   (c) What fraction is left? _____

   (d) What percentage is gone? _____

   (e) What percentage is left? _____

3.
   This box of biscuits contains 50 biscuits.
   12 are chocolate and the rest are plain.
   Fill in the missing numbers in this table.

| Chocolate | 12 | $\frac{12}{50} = \frac{\phantom{0}}{100}$ | 0.____ | ____ % |
| Plain | ____ | $\frac{\phantom{0}}{50} = \frac{\phantom{0}}{100}$ | 0.____ | ____ % |

4. Farmer Murphy had 200 animals on his farm.
   40% of them were sheep.
   How many sheep did he have? _____

5. Brian's Daddy won €500 in the lottery.
   He spent 90% of it on a new lawnmower.

   (a) How much was the lawnmower? €_____

   (b) How much had he left? €_____

# What is the name of this picture?

To find out the title of this picture you must work out the following problems and then match the letter that goes with each question with the answers in the grid below.

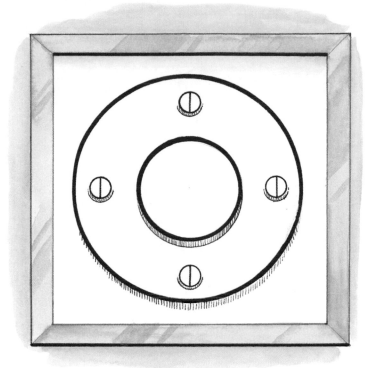

1. Find 20% of 360 (R) _____

2. 25% = $\frac{}{4}$ (E)

3. Michael spent 50% of his money.
   He had €4.75 left.
   How much did he have at
   the beginning? _____ (A)

4. 0.3 = _____% (H)

5. What % of this rectangle is coloured? _____ (T)

6. 10% of €25 = _____ (D)

7. 30% of 80 = _____ (O)

8. $\frac{3}{4}$ = _____% (K)

9. 25% of 2km = _____m (B)

10. Martina had €20. She spent €5.
    What percentage did she spend? _____ (N)

11. What percentage of 1000 is 100? _____ (S)

| 20% | 30% | 1 | 500m | 72 | €9.50 | 10% | 10% | €2.50 | 24 | 24 | 72 | 75% | 25% | 24 | 500m |
|-----|-----|---|------|----|-------|-----|-----|-------|----|----|----|-----|-----|----|----|
|     |     |   |      |    |       |     |     |       |    |    |    |     |     |    |    |

1. $\frac{5}{6} + \frac{3}{4} = $ _____

2. $\frac{2}{3} - \frac{1}{9} = $ _____

3. $2\frac{2}{3} + 1\frac{5}{6} = $ _____

4. $3\frac{1}{2} - 1\frac{3}{5} = $ _____

5. This small carton of orange juice contains $\frac{1}{4}$ of a litre. Siobhán brought one carton like this to school every day for a week.
How much orange juice did she drink during the week? _____ l _____ ml

6. How many hours and minutes are there between 10.30 a.m. and 1.45 p.m.? _____

7. Write 4.55 p.m. in twenty-four hour clock time. _____

8. Circle the earliest time: 1.50 p.m., 2.45 a.m. or 8.45 a.m.

9. The film 'Superkid' is 2 hours 23 minutes in length. If the last showing in the cinema finishes at 10.05 p.m. at what time does the film start? _____

10. This man went to bed at 23.50 and he set his clock to alarm 7 hours 15 minutes later. At what time did he set his alarm to go off? _____

11. Circle the object that has the greatest capacity.

a mug     a kettle     a sink

# Time to look back 5

12. Write 2l 855ml as litres using a decimal point. _____l

13. Find the difference between 4l 275ml and 1l 750ml. _____

14. This bottle contains 3 litres of water.
    If 956ml was used at lunch time and
    1l 275ml was used at dinner, how much
    water was be left in the bottle? _____

15. Circle the smallest amount:

   2l 125ml               2.2l                2$\frac{1}{10}$l

16. Colour 75% of this chocolate bar.

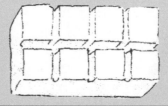

| 17. $\frac{3}{5}$ = _____ % | 18. 30% of 4 litres = _____ml | 19. $\frac{40}{100}$ = 0.4 = _____ % |
|---|---|---|

20. Catherine spent 75% of her €150 on a new jacket.
    How much money had she left? _____

How well did you do? Tick the box that shows your score.

|  |  |  |  |
|---|---|---|---|
| 18-20 | 15-17 | 10-14 | 0-9 |
| Excellent | Very Good | Good | Keep up the good work |

# Chapter 26
## 3-D Shapes

**You need:**
– 3-D shapes and a cereal box
– to revise vertices, edges and faces
– to explain tetrahedron
– to explain prism again

> A 3-D shape has three dimensions:
> length, width and height.

1. Match the shapes below with their correct names from this list.

hexagonal prism,   cuboid,   triangular pyramid,   sphere
square pyramid,   triangular prism,   cylinder,   cone
pentagonal prism,   hexagonal pyramid,   cube,   pentagonal pyramid.

(a)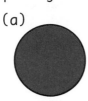

(b)

(c)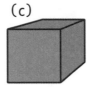

(d)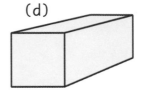

(e)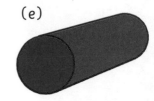

_____

(f)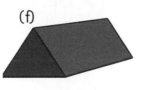

(g)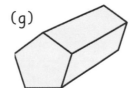

(h)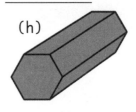

_____

(i)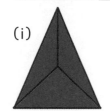

(j)

(k)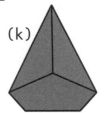

(l)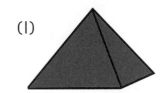

_____

2.

Pablo Picasso (1881–1973) and other famous artists sometimes used 3-D shapes in their paintings. This style of painting became known as Cubism. Look at this picture by an artist named Fernand Léger (1881–1955).
Can you see a few cylinders in the picture? Now draw or paint your own cubist style picture using as many 3-D shapes as you like.

# Looking back again

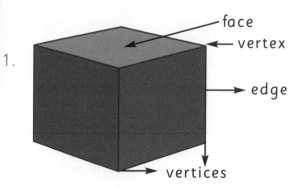

1.
face
vertex
edge
vertices

When a prism is cut into slices all the slices are the same shape as the original prism.

A cube has
(a) how many edges? _____
(b) how many vertices? _____
(c) how many faces? _____
(d) how is a cube a prism? _____

2. Write **Yes** or **No**.

A cube has

(a) a curved face _____   (b) a triangular face _____   (c) a circular face _____

(d) a square face _____   (e) a rectangular face _____   (f) a pentagonal face _____

(g) a hexagonal face _____

3. A cube has s_ _ s_ _ _ _ _ faces.

4. Name three 3-D shapes which have curved faces.

_____      _____      _____

5.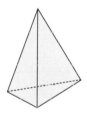

(a) A triangular pyramid is called a **tetrahedron**.

(b) A tetrahedron has _____ triangular faces, _____ edges and _____ vertices.

6. Fill in the grid. The first line is started for you.

| | No. of vertices | No. of edges | No. of faces | Shapes of faces |
|---|---|---|---|---|
| Cuboid | 8 | | | 2 square, 4 rectangular |
| Tetrahedron | | | | |
| Hexagonal pyramid | | | | |
| Square pyramid | | | | |
| Triangular prism | | | | |

# Nets of 3-D shapes

The net of a 3-D shape is what it looks like when it is opened out flat.

1.

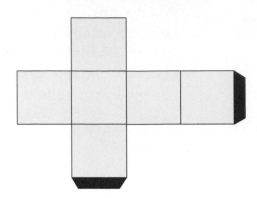

The red flaps help to hold the net together.

2. Here is another net of a cube. Draw three more nets of cubes in the boxes.

| (a) | (b) |
|-----|-----|
| | |
| (c) | (d) |
| | |

3.

(a) In Box A, draw what you think the net of a cereal box would look like.

(b) Now open out a cereal box and copy the net in Box B.

(c) Compare the two drawings.

| A |
|---|
| B |

# More nets of 3-D shapes

1. The following nets have been drawn without flaps because they will not be used to construct 3-D shapes.
   What 3-D shape does each of these nets represent?

(a)

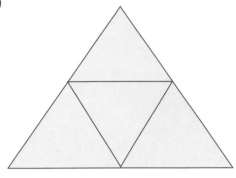

_____

(b)

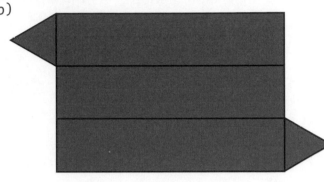

_____

(c)

_____

(d)

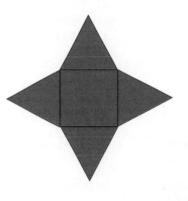

_____

(e)

_____

(f)

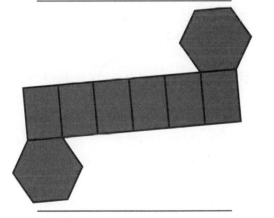

_____

2. How many flaps would be needed on each net to construct the 3-D shape?

   (a) _____   (b) _____   (c) _____   (d) _____   (e) _____   (f) _____

3. Make nets (with flaps) from light cardboard and construct
   (a) a cube, (b) a cuboid and (c) a tetrahedron.

# True or False?

1. A three-dimensional shape has length, width and height.

2. A two-dimensional shape has thickness.

3. A cube has only four vertices.

4. A cuboid has twelve edges.

5. A square pyramid has five faces.

6. A triangular prism has only five vertices.

7. A hexagonal pyramid has six triangular faces.

8. A pentagonal prism has only fourteen edges.

9. A cone has one square face.

10. A triangular pyramid is called a tetrahedron.

11. A tetrahedron has six edges.

12. A sphere has a curved surface.

13. A pentagonal pyramid has more faces than a hexagonal pyramid.

14. The six faces of a cube are equal in size.

15. A cuboid has more vertices than a cube.

16. The word 'vertices' is another word for 'corners'.

17. The plural of 'vertex' is 'vertices'.

18. A prism can be cut into slices which are the same shape as the original prism.

19. A square pyramid is a prism.

20. A cuboid is a prism.

SALE 25% off

€80

How m...
runners...

• To find...

  25% =

• $\frac{1}{4}$ of €8...

• There is...

• Sinéad w...
  (€80 – €20 = €60) Good Value !!

Sometimes goods...
than the full...
can be cal...
'the red...

All these items are reduced by 20%. Can you find their sale price?

€60

Computer game €30

€45

€6

€12
Paint set

70c

€1

MARKER'S €1.50

€160

€15

€75

MUSIC CD €7.50

SALE PRICES

1. Tracksuit _____

2. Computer game _____

3. Rugby jersey _____

4. Book _____

5. Painting set _____

6. Ruler _____

7. Pen _____

8. Packet of markers _____

9. Bicycle _____

10. Skateboard _____

11. Personal stereo _____

12. CD _____

# Reduced prices

...are sold at less
...price. This new price
...'the sale price',
...uced price', or 'the discount price'.

Put these words into sentences.

**...o discuss:**

- Why do shopkeepers have sales?

- What times of the year do they offer reductions on their prices?

- Why would you not get discounts on items coming up to Christmas?

1. Reduce these amounts by 10%.

   (a) €80 _____   (b) €90 _____   (c) €100 _____   (d) €120 _____

   (e) €45 _____   (f) €55 _____   (g) €75 _____   (h) €95 _____

2. Each of these items is reduced as shown. Find the sale price in each case.

   (a) T-shirt
   €25 – 10% off

   (b) Computer
   €890 – 30% off

   (c) TV
   €450 – 20% off

   (d) Kettle
   €50 – 40% off

   _____   _____   _____   _____

   (e) Child's desk
   €150 – 25% off

   (f) Flower vase
   €35 – 10% off

   (g) Box of chocolates
   €5.50 – 20% off

   (h) Tin of biscuits
   €8 – 20% off.

   _____   _____   _____   _____

# Problems for you to solve

1. A tour operator was offering a 10% discount for early booking on a holiday that cost €700.
How much would Mary's mother have to pay if she booked early? _____

2. A pair of runners was priced at €90. Paul got a discount of 20% at the sale after Christmas.
How much did he pay for the runners?_____

3. Ciara's Mum went to the garage to buy a new car.
The car she wanted was priced at €25 000.
The sales person said that he would give her a reduction of 10% if she paid cash (not a trade-in).

(a) How much of a reduction would she get?_____

(b) What was the cash price of the car? _____

4. Thomas bought this coat last summer. The marked price was €90.

(a) How much of a reduction did he get? _____

(b) What was the sale price? _____

5. The full price of this carpet was €250.
It was reduced by 30% in the January sales.

(a) By how much was the carpet reduced? _____

(b) What was the sale price? _____

# Increases

**Example**

The price of petrol went up by 10%
in the budget.
What is the new price?

$10\% = \frac{1}{10}$

$\frac{1}{10}$ of 90c = 9c

90c + 9c = 99c

New price = 99c

Petrol
90c per
Litre

**Discuss these:**

10% service charge

20% VAT

5% charge for packaging
and postage

10% commission

1. Increase these prices by the percentage shown beside each one.

   (a) Ruler 60c + 10%

   _____

   (b) Ice-cream 60c + 20%

   _____

   (c) CD €8 + 25%

   _____

   (d) Burger €1.20 + 20%

   _____

   (e) Tennis racket €30 + 25%

   _____

   (f) Book €6.50 + 10%

   _____

2. Increase:

   (a) 60c by 30% _____

   (b) 90m by 10% _____

   (c) 80kg by 40% _____

   (d) €7.20 by 50% _____

   (e) 90 litres by 60% _____

   (f) 25 players by 20% _____

3. By how much will each of the following items be increased?

   (a) Football socks
       €3.50 + 10%

   _____

   (b) Ice-cream
       €1.20 + 10%

   _____

   (c) Train ticket
       €7 + 25%

   _____

   (d) Children's allowance
       €75 + 20%

   _____

   (e) Daddy's wages
       €260 + 10%

   _____

   (f) Bag of coal
       €12 + 30%

   _____

   (g) Granny's pension
       €120 + 20%

   _____

   (h) Niamh's pocket money
       €6 + 10%

   _____

   (i) Price of copy
       36c + 25%

   _____

# Problems for you to solve

1. Tom's Daddy bought a new TV last Christmas for €495 but that price did not include the Value Added Tax of 20%.

   What price did he pay for the TV? _____

2. The price of the television licence increased by 10%. It was €110.

   (a) By how much did it increase? _____

   (b) What is the new price of the licence? _____

3. The number of people out of work last year was 98,000, but it increased by 20% this year. How many people are out of work this year? _____

4. Mrs Black bought a new washing machine for €280 but there was a 20% charge for delivery and fitting. What was the total cost of the washing machine? _____

5. Jamie's Dad is a car salesperson. Every time he sells a car he gets a commission of 10%.
   Last week he sold a Toyota car for €26 500.
   How much commission did he get? _____

6. Last year Western Bank made a profit of €155 million but this year the profits increased by 40%.

   (a) By how much did the profits increase? €_____

   (b) How much profit did they make this year? €_____

7. By how much is 25% of €960 greater than 35% of €750? €_____

# Increase and decrease with calculators

Percentage increases or decreases can be calculated very easily by using a calculator.

## Example 1

The shopkeeper reduced the price of a CD player by 30%. Find the sale price.

Key in  **2 5 0 − 3 0 %**

Ans: = €175 (sale price)

## Example 2

Paula's Dad was earning €350 a week. Last week he got a 10% increase. How much does he earn now?

Key in  **3 5 0 + 1 0 %**

Ans: = €385 (new wage)

Do these with your calculator.

1. Reduce:
   (a) €35 by 20% _____
   (b) €7.50 by 30% _____
   (c) 90c by 10% _____

   (d) 2kg by 25% _____
   (e) 3 metres by 40% _____
   (f) 3l by 60% _____

   (g) $2\frac{1}{2}$ kg by 10% _____
   (h) 75c by 20% _____
   (i) $1\frac{1}{2}$ hours by 10% _____

2. Increase:
   (a) 75 by 10% _____
   (b) 65 by 40% _____
   (c) 90 by 55% _____

   (d) €8.50 by 30% _____
   (e) €75 by 60% _____
   (f) €150 by 75% _____

   (g) $3\frac{1}{2}$ kg by 20% _____
   (h) 90cm by 40% _____
   (i) $2\frac{1}{2}$ hours by 70% _____

3. Find the price of this bicycle when tax is added on. _____

4. A pair of runners priced at €96 was reduced by 20%.
   (a) The runners were reduced by € _____
   (b) What was the sale price? _____

€295 + 21% VAT

# A Daring Escape

Each room in this maze contains an answer – but only 14 of them are the correct answers to the questions below. When you find a correct answer in a room put a circle around it. You can use these as stepping stones to the next room. Keep working until you find a path to the treasure. Then make your escape along this trail. Colour it in to help future warriors who may go in search of buried treasure. Good luck!

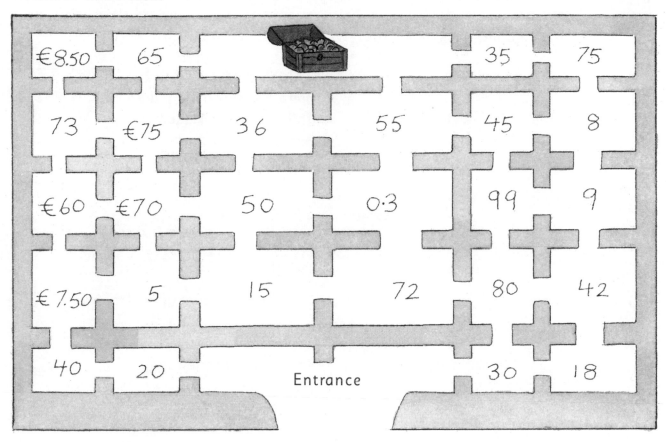

1. $\frac{3}{4}$ = _____ %

2. $\frac{2}{5}$ = _____ %

3. 0.8 = _____ %

4. 10% of €75 = € _____

5. 20% of €40 = € _____

6. Increase 40 by 25% = _____

7. Decrease 70 by 50% _____

8. €60 + 20% VAT = € _____

9. 10% discount on a T-Shirt priced €50. Find the new price. €_____

10. Reduce €100 by 30% _____

11. The price of petrol increased by 10%. It was 90c a litre. How much now? _____ c

12. 30% = _____

13. 20% = [1]

14. 20% of €1 = _____ c

## Chapter 28
### Area

**You need:**
– 4 metre sticks or 4 pieces of card 1 metre in length
– measuring tape or trundle wheel
– string 1 metre long

## A  Looking back

> **We use the word 'area' to describe the size of a surface.**

1. Measure the length of the four sides of this square.

   Each side is _____ in length.

   The area of this square is 1 square centimetre = 1 sq. cm or 1cm².

2. Now put four metre sticks or four 1 metre lengths of card on the floor like this.

   Each side of this square is 1 metre in length. The area of this square is 1 square metre = 1 sq. m or 1m².

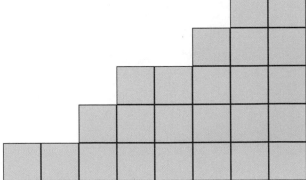

1 metre

1 metre

1 metre

1 metre

> **We measure area in cm² or m².**

3. Would you use cm² or m² to measure the area of the following:
   (a) the cover of a copybook _____
   (b) the floor of the classroom _____
   (c) playground _____
   (d) the surface of your desk/table _____
   (e) playing card _____
   (f) football pitch _____
   (g) page of your history book _____
   (h) page of a newspaper _____
   (i) carpark _____
   (j) garden _____

4. Look at these shapes. They are made up of cm².
   (i)                                   (ii)

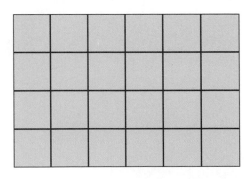

   (a) Which shape do you think has the larger area?

   (b) Estimate the area of both shapes in cm². _____
       Shape (i) _____    Shape (ii) _____

   (c) Find the actual area of both shapes by counting the cm² in each.
       Shape (i) _____    Shape (ii) _____

166

# Find the area of shapes

1. This diagram shows the tiled area of a hotel foyer. Each tile is 1m².

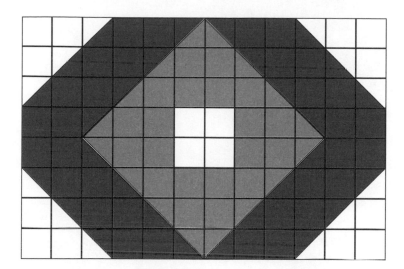

(a) Estimate the area of the foyer.

_____m²

(b) Estimate the area of
   (i)  the light blue tiles _____m²
   (ii) the navy tiles _____m²
   (iii) the white tiles _____m²

(c) Now count the squares to find
   the area of the
   (i)  light blue tiles _____m²
   (ii) navy tiles _____m²
   (iii) white tiles _____m²

(d) Use the information in (c) to find the total area of the foyer. _____m²

2. Look at this shape. Each small square has an area of 1cm².

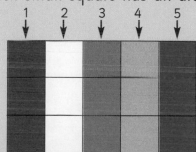

(a) Measure the length and width of the rectangle.

Length = _____cm          Width = _____cm

(b) How many columns can you see? _____

(c) How many cm² in each column? _____

(d) There are 5 columns with 3 cm² in each.
   Therefore the area of the rectangle = 5 x 3 cm² =_____cm².

(e) Now count the cm² to find the area. _____cm²

(f) Now look at the length and width of the rectangle which you wrote in (a) and you may notice something interesting!

# Area of rectangles

**A   Moving on**

1.   Each square in this rectangle is 1cm².

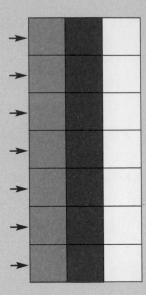

(a) Length = _____ cm     Width = _____ cm

(b) Area of rectangle = _____ rows of _____ cm²

   = _____ x _____ cm² = _____ cm².

(c) Count the cm² in the rectangle to see if answer (b) is correct.

(d) You have probably noticed that if you multiply the length of the rectangle by its width you will find the area of the rectangle. Try it now.

Area of the rectangle = L x W = _____ cm x _____ cm = _____ cm².

To find the area of a rectangle multiply the length by the width (L x W).

2.   Now find the area of these rectangles.

(a)

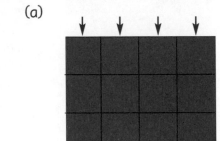

(b)

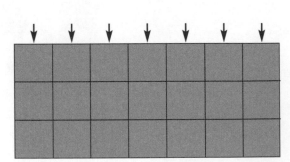

(i)   How many columns? _____

(ii)  How many cm² in each column? _____cm²

(iii) What is the area of the rectangle?

_____ columns x _____cm² = _____cm²

L x W = _____ x_____ = _____ cm²

(i)   How many columns? _____

(ii)  How many cm² in each column? ____cm²

(iii) What is the area of the rectangle?

_____ columns x _____ cm² = _____cm²

L x W = _____ x_____ = _____ cm²

# Area of rectangles

1. Find the area of each rectangle.

(a)

(b)

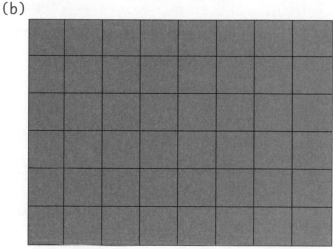

L x W = _____ cm  x _____ cm  = _____ c m²   L x W = _____ cm  x _____ cm  = _____ c m²

(c)

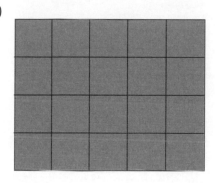

(d)

L x W = _____ cm  x _____ cm  = _____ c m²   L x W = _____ cm  x _____ cm  = _____ c m²

Now count the cm² in each rectangle and check your answers.

2. (a) Draw these rectangles on cm² paper.
    (i) L = 6 cm, W = 5cm           (ii) L = 7 cm, W = 6 cm

    (iii) L = 8 cm, W = 7 cm        (iv) L = 10 cm, W = 5 cm

(b) Use your calculator to find the area of each rectangle.

    Area (i) _____      (ii) _____      (iii) _____      (iv) _____

(c) Now count the number of c m² in each rectangle to check your answers.

# Area of a square

Look at this diagram of a kitchen floor. The owner of the house wants to buy new flooring which measures 6 metres in length and 6 metres in width.
Flooring is sold by the square metre so the owner needs to find the area of his kitchen floor.
(Each cm² stands for 1 metre.)

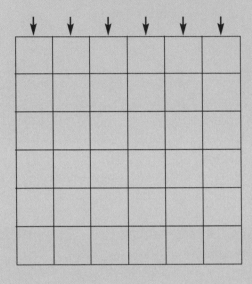

(a) What shape is the floor? _____

(b) How many columns can you see? _____

How many sq. metres in each column? _____

How many sq. metres altogether? _____

(c) Length of square = _____m

Width of square = _____m

Area of square = L x W = _____ x _____ = _____m²

(d) Check your answer using a calculator.

Now find the area of the following shapes and check your answers using a calculator.

1. Find the area of these squares.

(a) Side 9cm. Area = _____      (b) Side 5m. Area = _____

(c) Side 7cm. Area = _____      (d) Side 6m. Area = _____

(e) Side 4.5cm. Area = _____      (f) Side 7.5m. Area = _____

2. Find the area of these rectangles.

(a) 18cm long, 5cm wide. Area = _____      (b) 26m long, 6m wide. Area = _____

(c) 15cm long, 9cm wide. Area = _____      (d) 33m long, 7m wide. Area = _____

(e) 16cm long, 8.5cm wide. Area = _____ (f) 26m long, 12.5m wide. Area = _____

# Problems for you to solve

1. Part of this school was decorated during the holidays.
   The classrooms measure 12 metres in length and 8 metres
   in width, and the PE hall measures 24 metres in length and
   15 metres in width.

   (a) Find the area of one classroom. _____

   (b) New carpet costing €25 per square metre was laid in four classrooms.
       Find the cost of the new carpeting for

       (i) one classroom _____        (ii) all four classrooms _____

   (c) The wooden floor of the PE hall was sanded and varnished at a cost of
       €12 per square metre. How much did this work cost? _____

   (d) How much money altogether was spent on decorating the school
       during the holidays? _____

   (e) Check your answers using a calculator.

2. The sides of each square on the chessboard in the
   picture are 4cm in length.

   (a) Find out how many squares there are on
       a chessboard. _____

   (b) What is the area of each square? _____

   (c) Find the total area of the white squares. _____

   (d) What area is covered by the black squares? _____

   (e) What is the area of the board? _____

   (f) What is the perimeter of the playing area
       of the board? _____

3. This sitting room is 6 metres long and 4 metres wide.
   How many square metres of carpet are needed to
   cover the floor if the fireplace is 2 metres wide and
   1 metre deep? _____

   1m  Fireplace
           2m
   4m

   6m

# Finding the area of irregular shapes

**Example 1**

(a)

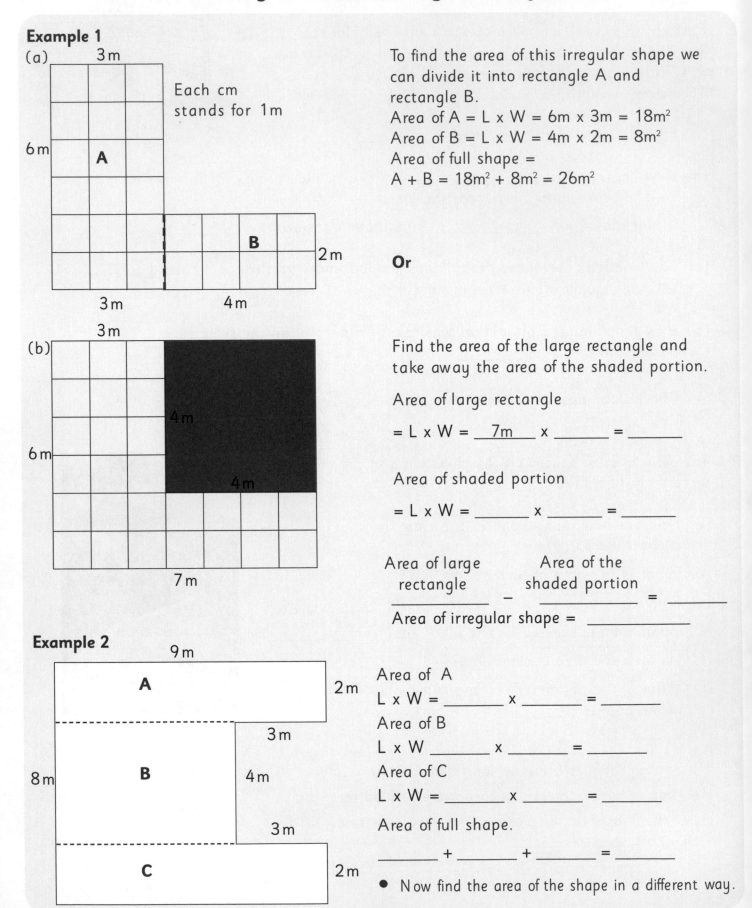

To find the area of this irregular shape we can divide it into rectangle A and rectangle B.

Area of A = L x W = 6m x 3m = 18m²
Area of B = L x W = 4m x 2m = 8m²
Area of full shape =
A + B = 18m² + 8m² = 26m²

**Or**

(b)

Find the area of the large rectangle and take away the area of the shaded portion.

Area of large rectangle

= L x W = ___7m___ x _____ = _____

Area of shaded portion

= L x W = _____ x _____ = _____

| Area of large rectangle | | Area of the shaded portion | |
|---|---|---|---|

_____ − _____ = _____
Area of irregular shape = _____

**Example 2**

Area of A
L x W = _____ x _____ = _____
Area of B
L x W _____ x _____ = _____
Area of C
L x W = _____ x _____ = _____
Area of full shape.

_____ + _____ + _____ = _____

• Now find the area of the shape in a different way.

172

# Area of irregular shapes

1. Find the area of these irregular shapes.
   Check your answers using a calculator.

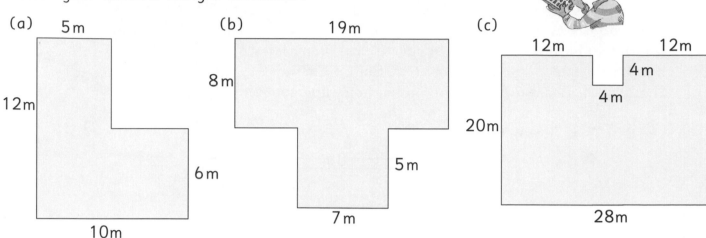

(a) 5m
   12m
   10m
   6m

   Area = _____

(b) 19m
   8m
   7m
   5m

   Area = _____

(c) 12m   12m
   4m
   4m
   20m
   28m

   Area = _____

2. Find the areas of these shapes.

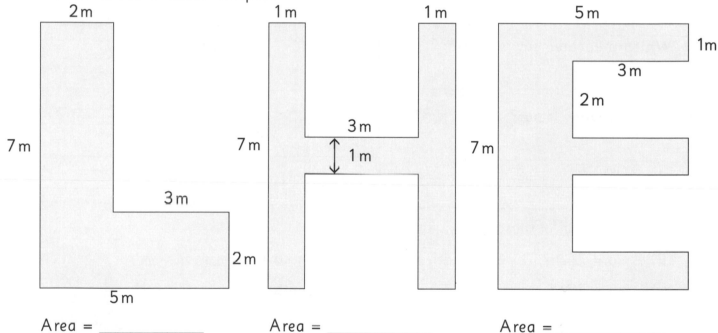

   2m
   7m
   3m
   2m
   5m

   Area = _____

   1m   1m
   7m
   3m
   1m

   Area = _____

   5m
   1m
   3m
   2m
   7m

   Area = _____

**Time to measure**

3. Now your teacher will help you to choose a space in your school and you can find its area. Use a trundle wheel to find the length and width of each space to the nearest metre.

4. Use a measuring tape or a 1-metre length of string to find the length and width to the nearest metre of two rooms in your home.
   (a) Area of Room 1 _____   (b) Area of Room 2_____
   (c) Find the cost of carpeting one room if carpet costs €28 per square metre._____
   (d) Find the cost of laying a wooden floor in the other room if the flooring costs €35 per square metre. _____

# A puzzle ...

1. A teacher gave his fifth class this question as homework. The area of a room is 56m². The room is 8m long. **How wide is the room?** Here is how one girl worked it out. If the room was 8m in length, she knew that this is how the length would look. Then she wondered how many lines of 8m² would make up an area of 56m². 56m² ÷ 8m = 7m. She drew a diagram of the room in her copy and counted the squares and she knew she had the correct answer. L = 8m, W = 7m. Area = 56m²

← ———————————— 8 m ———————————— →

| Area of a rectangle or square ÷ L = W. | Area of a rectangle or square ÷ W = L. |

This is a drawing of a tennis court.

**Which measurement is missing?**

_____

Can you work it out?

_____

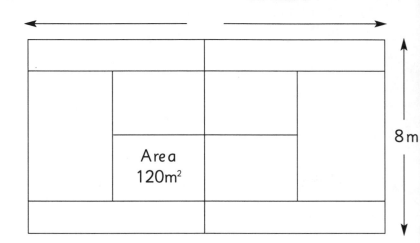

Area 120m²

8 m

2. Find the length of these rectangles if:

   (a) Area = 24cm²,      Width = 4cm,      Length = _____

   (b) Area = 70m²,      Width = 7m,      Length = _____

   (c) Area = 136 cm²,      Width = 8cm,      Length = _____

   (d) Area = 216m²,      Width = 9m,      Length = _____

3. Find the width of these rectangles if:

   (a) Area = 54m²,      Length = 9m,      Width = _____

   (b) Area = 72m²,      Length = 9m,      Width = _____

   (c) Area = 132m²,      Length = 12m,      Width = _____

   (d) Area = 210cm²,      Length = 15cm,      Width = _____

4. Check the answers in Questions 2 and 3 using a calculator.

# Go for it!

1. Look at the diagrams of two gardens below. Each square represents a square metre.

(A) 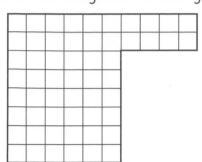    (B)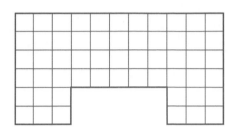

(a) Which garden, do you think, has the greater area? _____

(b) Estimate the area of each garden. A _____    B _____

(c) Now find the actual area of each garden.  A _____    B _____

2. This diagram shows a park with a 2m wide path around a grass area. There are three square flowerbeds of the same size in the grass patch.

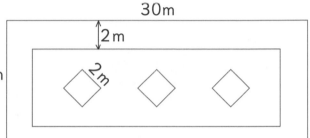

(a) Find the total area of the park. _____

(b) Find the area of the three flowerbeds. _____

(c) What area is covered by grass? _____

(d) Find the cost of sowing grass seed at €15 per square metre. _____

(e) What is the area of the path? _____

(f) What would it cost to pave the path at €36 per square metre? _____

(g) Check your answers using a calculator.

3. It cost €1,440 to carpet the sitting room in this house. The carpet was €30 per square metre.

(a) Find the area of the sitting room. _____

(b) If the sitting room was 8 metres in length, what was the width of the room? _____

**You need:**
- protractors
- to explain data, sector, rotations
- to revise averages

## A   Bar charts

1.  Here is a bar chart showing the weights of Emma, Paul, Mary and Jack.

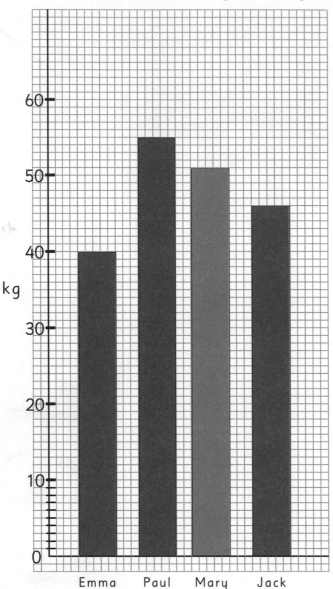

Fill in the missing numbers.

Emma: _____ kg

Paul: _____ kg

Mary: _____ kg

Jack: _____ kg

Total weight: _____ kg

Divide the total weight by 4 to find the average weight of the 4 children.

Average weight: _____ kg.

(a) Draw a line across the graph showing the average weight of the 4 children.

(b) Which children are above the average weight? _____ , _____

(c) How would you describe Jack's weight? _____

(d) Is Emma above or below the average weight? _____

(e) By how much is Paul heavier than Emma? _____

(f) By how much is Jack lighter than Paul? _____

# Line graphs

1.  Here is a line graph showing the 5 favourite sports of the pupils in fifth class in Longmile National School.

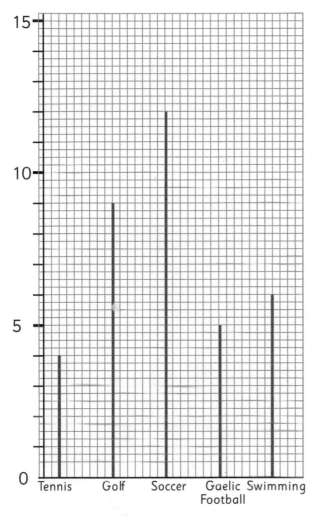

Fill in the missing numbers.

Tennis: _____ pupils

Golf: _____ pupils

Soccer: _____ pupils

Gaelic football: _____ pupils

Swimming: _____ pupils

Total: _____ pupils

(a) Which is the most popular sport? _____

(b) Which is the least popular sport? _____

(c) How many more pupils prefer soccer to Gaelic football? _____

(d) How many less prefer swimming to golf? _____

(e) What percentage of the class prefered golf? _____

2.  (a) Find out the 5 favourite sports of the children in your class and then in your copy draw a line graph to show this data.

(b) Write 3 questions about the graph and see if your friend can find the answers.

# Pie charts

## 1. Woeful and Wonderful

These pie-charts show the results of the best team and the worst team in the league. Each team played 40 games.

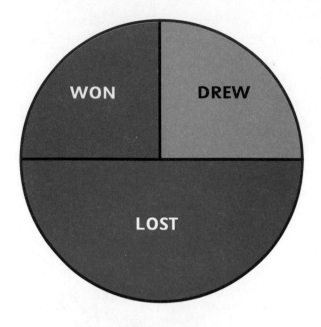

This pie chart shows the results of Woeful United – the team at the bottom of the league.

- How many games did Woeful lose? _____
- How many did they win? _____
- How many did they draw? _____
- If there are 2 points for a win and 1 point for a draw, how many points did they get? _____

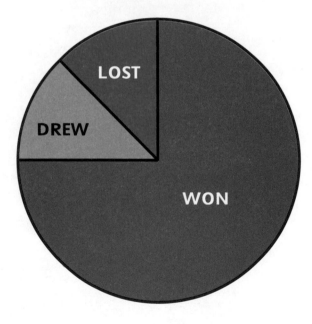

This pie chart shows the results of Wonderful City – the best team in the league.

- How many games did they win? _____
- How many did they lose? _____
- How many games did they draw? _____
- How many points did they get? _____

## 2. Brian's homework

Last night Brian spent 2 hours doing his homework. He spent 1 hour doing mathematics, 45 minutes doing Irish and 15 minutes doing English.
Draw a pie chart to show this data.
Then write 3 questions about the pie chart.

# Multiple bar charts

1. This table and the bar chart show the amount of money raised by the Parents' Association in St Michael's School in 2001 and in 2002.

| Year | Coffee morning | Concert | Sponsored walk | Christmas raffle | Sale of work |
|------|----------------|---------|----------------|------------------|--------------|
| 2001 | €700 | €600 | €550 | €650 | €450 |
| 2002 | €800 | €550 | €500 | €750 | €500 |

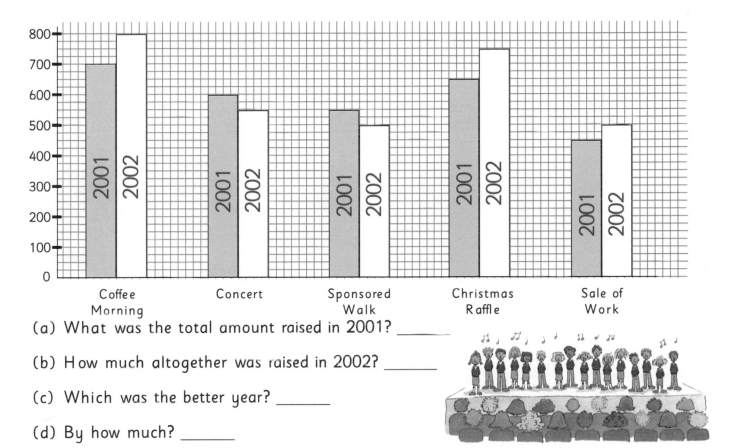

(a) What was the total amount raised in 2001? _____

(b) How much altogether was raised in 2002? _____

(c) Which was the better year? _____

(d) By how much? _____

2. The following table shows the attendance of the children of fifth and sixth class in Millbrook National School over a week. There are 40 pupils in each class. In your copy show this data on a **multiple bar chart.**

| Class | Mon | Tues | Wed | Thur | Fri |
|-------|-----|------|-----|------|-----|
| 5th | 35 | 30 | 40 | 35 | 30 |
| 6th | 40 | 30 | 35 | 35 | 35 |

(a) What is the average attendance of fifth class? _____

(b) What is the average attendance of sixth class? _____

(c) Which class has the best attendance? ____

(d) The highest attendance was on _____ _____

(e) The lowest attendance was on _____

# Pie charts

**A sector is a part of a circle.**

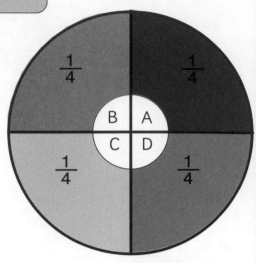

- Look at this circle. It is divided into 4 sectors. Each sector is $\frac{1}{4}$ of the circle. The angles A, B, C, D are 90° ($\frac{1}{4}$ of 360°) (360° is a full rotation) Now use your protractor to check the measure of the 4 angles.

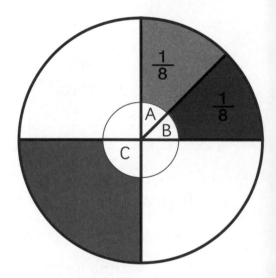

- Now look at this circle.
  What fraction of the circle is coloured blue? _____
  What fraction of the circle is red? _____
  Now take your protractor and measure the angle at A.
  How many degrees in angle A? _____
  How many degrees in angle B? _____
  What fraction is coloured green? _____
  How big is angle C? _____

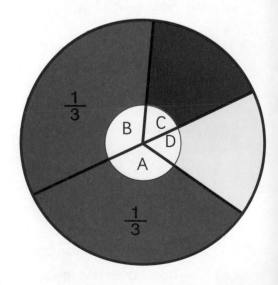

- Now look at this circle.
  What fraction is coloured green? _____
  Now measure the angle at A.
  How many degrees in angle A? _____
  $\frac{1}{3}$ of 360° = _____
  How many degrees is B? _____
  How many degrees is C? _____
  How many degrees is D? _____
  What fraction is coloured red? _____
  What fraction is coloured yellow? _____

# Constructing pie charts

**Example**

The 40 children in fifth class in St Brendan's School were asked how they came to school every morning.

| Transport | Walk | Bus | Car | Bicycle |
|---|---|---|---|---|
| Number of children | 20 | 10 | 5 | 5 |

- 20 out of 40 children walked, so $\frac{1}{2}$ of them walked to school.
$\frac{1}{2}$ of 360° = 180°. This is a straight angle.

- 10 came by bus. 10 out of 40 is $\frac{10}{40} = \frac{1}{4}$.
So $\frac{1}{4}$ of the children came on the bus.
$\frac{1}{4}$ of 360° = 90°.

- 5 came by car. $\frac{5}{40} = \frac{1}{8}$.
So $\frac{1}{8}$ of the children came in the car.
$\frac{1}{8}$ of 360° = 45°.

- 5 also came on bicycles. $\frac{5}{40} = \frac{1}{8}$.
So $\frac{1}{8}$ of the children came to school by bicycle.
$\frac{1}{8}$ of 360° = 45°.

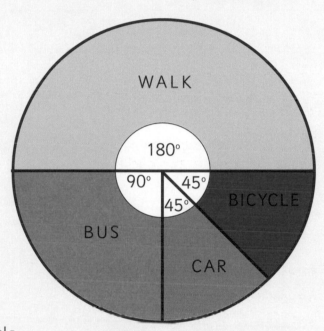

- Which is the most popular way of coming to school? _____

This table shows the favourite pastimes of 24 children in Millmount Youth Club.

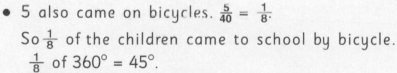

| Pastimes | TV | Football | Music | Reading |
|---|---|---|---|---|
| Children | | | | |

Draw a pie chart to show this information.

# More pie charts

### Example

A group of 30 children were asked which
of the following makes of car they preferred:
Ford, Toyota, Opel, Renault.

| Cars | Ford | Toyota | Opel | Renault |
|------|------|--------|------|---------|
| Children | 10 | 10 | 5 | 5 |

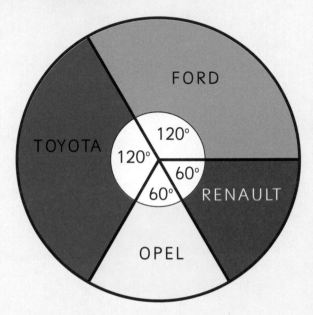

- 10 out of 30 children preferred Ford. $\frac{10}{30} = \frac{1}{3}$
  $\frac{1}{3}$ of 360° = 120°.
  We draw an angle of 120°.

- 10 children also prefer Toyota, so we draw
  an angle of 120° this time as well.

- 5 children prefer Opel. $\frac{5}{30} = \frac{1}{6}$
  $\frac{1}{6}$ of 360° = 60°.
  Now we draw an angle of 60°.

- 5 children also prefer Renault.
  The angle for the Renault is also 60°.
  This angle is already drawn.

This table shows the amount of pocket money that Niall, Shane,
Aoife and Aisling get every week.

| Children | Niall | Shane | Aoife | Aisling |
|----------|-------|-------|-------|---------|
| Pocket money | €12 | €6 | €6 | €12 |

Draw a pie chart to show this data.

What is the average amount of money that each child gets? _____

# More charts for you to draw

1. Farmer O'Neill has 80 animals on his farm.
   He has 20 cows, 40 sheep, 10 pigs and 10 horses.
   In your copy draw a table to show this information
   and then construct a pie chart of the data.

2. The hair colours of the children in 5th class in Westbrook School are as follows:
   Brown hair 8, Black hair 10, Red hair 5, Fair hair 7.
   Draw a table to show this information and then represent your findings on a bar chart.

3. (a) With the help of your teacher, choose the 5 most popular TV programmes.

   Ask each child which is their preferred
   programme and record the answers
   on a piece of paper.
   Draw a table of your findings.

   Then construct a bar chart to show this information.

   Write 3 questions about the survey.

   (b) Now ask each child which of the following 4 school subjects that they prefer:

   ENGLISH, MATHEMATICS, HISTORY, GEOGRAPHY.

   Then draw a table of the answers and show the information on a pie chart.

   Write 3 questions about the survey.

4. Now ask your classmates about some of the following and draw a
   table and a suitable chart each time.

   (a) 4 favourite pop bands          (b) 5 favourite drinks

   (c) 4 most popular cereals          (d) 4 favourite fruits

   (e) 4 favourite colours              (f) 4 favourite animals

# Chapter 30

## Number Sentences

You need:
- a calculator

Here is a word sentence: 'I am in fifth class.'

Here is another word sentence but there is a missing word:

'My name is [                    ].' Can you fill in the missing word?

Here is a number sentence: 5 + 6 = 11

Here is a number sentence that has a missing number: 5 + [ ] = 14.

Can you fill in the missing number?

1. Fill in the missing numbers in these number sentences.

(a) 6 + [ ] = 15

(b) 8 + [ ] = 20

(c) 12 + [ ] = 28

(d) [ ] + 13 = 30

(e) [ ] + 14 = 25

(f) [ ] + 20 = 35

(g) 16 + 14 = [ ]

(h) 28 + 14 = [ ]

(i) 24 + 25 = [ ]

(j) 32 – [ ] = 12

(k) 40 – [ ] = 15

(l) 65 – [ ] = 50

(m) [ ] x 5 = 40

(n) 6 x [ ] = 30

(o) [ ] x 9 = 54

(p) 36 ÷ [ ] = 4

(q) 42 ÷ [ ] = 6

(r) [ ] ÷ 5 = 9

2. Fill in the missing symbols (+, –, x or ÷) in these number sentences.

(a) 6 [ ] 8 = 14

(b) 32 [ ] 20 = 12

(c) 6 [ ] 9 = 54

(d) 50 [ ] 32 = 18

(e) 28 [ ] 7 = 4

(f) 48 [ ] 8 = 6

(g) 7 [ ] 8 = 56

(h) 5 [ ] 9 = 45

(i) 100 [ ] 32 = 68

(j) 96 [ ] 8 = 12

(k) 15 [ ] 7 = 105

(l) 132 [ ] 4 = 33

184

# Number sentences

**Look at this word story.**

Michelle bought 6 writing copies in the school shop on Monday.
On Tuesday she bought another 8 writing copies.
How many writing copies did she buy altogether? _____

Here is the same story written as a number sentence.

$6 + 8 = \boxed{\phantom{00}}$

Have you worked out the missing number that goes in the box? _____

Here is another word story.
Shane spent €24 on 4 books. How much was each book? _____

That story written as a number sentence is

€24 ÷ 4 = € $\boxed{\phantom{00}}$

What number fits in the frame? _____

1. Write a number sentence to match each of these word stories and then
   find the answers.

   (a) There are 12 sweets in a pack. How many are in 7 packs? _____

   (b) Oisín got 62 marks in his Maths test but Eoin got 18 marks more than that.
       How many marks did Eoin get? _____

   (c) An egg producer wants to pack 144 eggs
       into boxes of 6.
       How many boxes does he need? _____

   (d) Maurice got €72 for his last birthday.
       He got €16 less than that on his
       previous birthday.
       How much money did he get then?_____

(e) A teacher shared 56 colouring pencils among 7 children.
    How many pencils did each child receive? _____

# More number sentences

1. Now write number sentences to match these word stories.

   (a) $\frac{1}{4}$ of Paul's cards are about football. If he has 12 football cards, how many cards has he got altogether? $\frac{1}{4}$ x ☐ = 12

   (b) Roisín spends 50% of her spare time every week watching television. If she watches television for $3\frac{1}{2}$ hours, how much spare time does she have? $3\frac{1}{2}$ x ☐ = ☐

   (c) When Tom had given 46c to Liam he had 20c left. How much money did he have before he gave any to Liam? ☐ – 46c = 20c

   (d) 25% of Denise's money is €3.50. How much money does she have?_____

   (e) Grace bought 4 rulers for €1.20. How much did she pay for each ruler?_____

2. In your copy write word stories for each of the following number sentences. The first one is done to help you.

   (a) ☐ + 16 = 40. When Joseph got 16 marbles from his friend Niamh, he then had 40. How many marbles did he have at first? _____

   (b) 28 + ☐ = 42   (c) 6 x 7 = ☐   (d) 32 ÷ ☐ = 8   (e) 60 – ☐ = 36

3. You can use your calculator to fill in these frames.

   (a) 360 + ☐ = 725

   (b) ☐ x 7 = 588

   (c) 95 ÷ ☐ = 19

   (d) ☐ – 465 = 942.

   **Remember!**

   ☐ x 3 = 45. To find the number in the frame it may be easier to divide even though there is a multiplication symbol in the question. So the missing number is 45 ÷ 3 = 15.
   The same applies when there is a +, – or ÷ symbol.

   (e) $\frac{1}{4}$ of ☐ = 20

   (f) 50% of ☐ = 64

   (g) 162.5 – ☐ = 86.2

   (h) ☐ – €16.25 = €9.50

   (i) $\frac{1}{4}$ of 96 = ☐

   (j) ☐ x 6 = 162

   (k) ☐ x 100 = 375

   (l) 16.2 + 2.94 = ☐

   (m) ☐ – 95 = 84

# Brackets

Can you work out the answer to this question? 3 + 7 x 4.

What answer did you get? _____

Did everybody in the class get the same answer? _____

In fact, there are 2 possible answers. It all depends whether you **add or multiply first.**

If you add first you get:
3 + 7 = 10. Then 10 x 4 = 40.
Ans: 40.

If you multiply first you get:
7 x 4 = 28. Then 3 + 28 = 31.
Ans: 31.

1. Now look at these questions and work out how many possible answers each question has.

   (a) 8 − 6 + 1 _____

   (b) 9 + 3 − 1 _____

   (c) 6 x 5 + 4 _____

   (d) 5 x 9 − 6 _____

   (e) 5 + 6 + 4 _____

   (f) 24 ÷ 4 − 3 _____

   (g) 2 x 5 x 3 _____

   (h) 48 ÷ 6 ÷ 2 _____

   (i) 12 − 7 − 2 _____

   (j) Which of the questions have 2 answers? _____

   (k) Which have only 1 answer? _____

   (l) Have you any idea as to why some questions have only 1 answer? _____

To avoid confusion we use brackets. Brackets tell us what to do first. We do the operations between the brackets first.

**Examples:**

   (a) (12 + 8) − 5
       = 20 − 5
       = 15
       Ans 15.

   (b) 6 x (5 − 4)
       = 6 x 1
       = 6
       Ans: 6

   (c) (12 ÷ 3) − 2
       = 4 − 2
       = 2
       Ans: 2.

2. Now try these.

   (a) (3 + 7) − 2 _____

   (b) 6 x (8 − 5) _____

   (c) (9 ÷ 3) − 1 _____

   (d) (16 − 8) + 6 _____

   (e) (38 + 6) − 13 _____

   (f) 100 − (50 − 25) _____

3. You may use your calculator to do these.

   (a) (96 − 48) + 24. _____

   (b) 274 + (66 − 51) _____

   (c) (140 x 2) − 65 _____

   (d) (48 ÷ 3) − 16 _____

   (e) 67 − (32 x 2) _____

   (f) (48 ÷ 4) ÷ 6 _____

# Which comes first?

Look at this question: 16 + 9 − 8 x 2. Should you add, subtract or multiply first? Discuss it with your partner or friend.

When brackets are not used in a question, multiplication and division must always be done before addition and subtraction.

Of course, if there are brackets also, the operation between the brackets must be done even before multiplication and division.

**Example 1**
(12 + 18) − 8 x 4 ÷ 2 (Brackets first 12 + 18)
= 30 − 8 x 4 ÷ 2 (Then multiply 8 x 4)
= 30 − 32 ÷ 2 (Now divide 32 ÷ 2)
= 30 − 16 (Then subtract 30 − 16)
= 14.

**Example 2**
6 x 9 ÷ 3 + 6 + (9 − 3)
= 6 x 9 ÷ 3 + 6 + 6
= 54 ÷ 3 + 6 + 6
= 18 + 6 + 6
= 18 + 12
= 30

Don't forget that **brackets** are first, following by **multiplication**, then **division**, then **addition** and last of all comes **subtraction**.

This sentence should help you to remember that rule:

B RUNO, MY DOG, ALWAYS SITS

Now try these. Bruno will help you.

(a)  15 x 6 ÷ 9 + 18 = _____

(b)  24 + 18 − 6 x 9 ÷ 3 = _____

(c)  96 − 48 ÷ 3 x 4 + 14 = _____

(d)  48 ÷ 2 + 13 − 6 + 4 = _____

(e)  (39 + 48) − 45 + 6 x 5 = _____

(f)  9 x 8 + 44 − 32 ÷ 8 = _____

(g)  48 x 26 ÷ (8 x 4) − 2 = _____

(h)  (72 − 16) + 84 ÷ 3 x 7 = _____

(i)  64 ÷ 4 + 74 − 18 x 2 = _____

(j)  7 x 10 ÷ 2 − 6 + 8 = _____

# Operation Bruno

Look at the questions below. After each question there is a letter. Put these letters in the boxes with the answers and see if you can crack the coded message. You may use your calculator, and don't forget Bruno.

BRUNO, **M**Y **D**OG, **A**LWAYS **S**ITS

(a) 640 + 96 ÷ 8 – 60   (O) _____

(b) 54 x 29 – (104 + 16)   (C) _____

(c) 940 – 96 + 84 ÷ (7 x 4)   (V) _____

(d) 217 ÷ 7 + 16 – 5 x 9   (R) _____

(e) 16 x 196 ÷ 4 + 18 x 37   (T) _____

(f) 48 x 16.5 + 320 – (9 x 72)   (I) _____

(g) (28 x 45) – (756 ÷ 18) + 19   (W) _____

(h) 976 ÷ 8 + 19 x 26 – 304   (S) _____

| 1199 | 97 | 583 | 464 | 312 | 1450 | 241 | 121 |
|------|-----|------|------|------|------|------|------|
|      |     |      |      |      |      |      |      |

| 1446 | 825 | 1493 | 841 | 845 | 2 | 360 | 592 | 416 |
|------|------|------|------|------|-----|------|------|------|
|      |      |      |      |      |     |      |      |      |

(i) (394 – 96) + 59 x 6 ÷ 3 =   (G) _____

(j) (56 x 16) – (364 ÷ 7) + 19 =   (L) _____

(k) 765 ÷ 17 + 98 – 2.75 x 8 =   (E) _____

(l) 640 + 56 – 96 + (136 ÷ 8) =   (O) _____

(m) 960 – 110 + 120 ÷ (6 x 4) =   (E) _____

(n) 720 ÷ 15 + 760 – 9 x 63 =   (H) _____

(o) (29 x 56) – (1045 ÷ 19) + 76 =   (E) _____

(p) 480 ÷ 3 + 648 – (8 x 56) =   (D) _____

(q) (964 – 396) – (387 + 68) + 16 =   (H) _____

# Chapter 31

## Time to look back 6

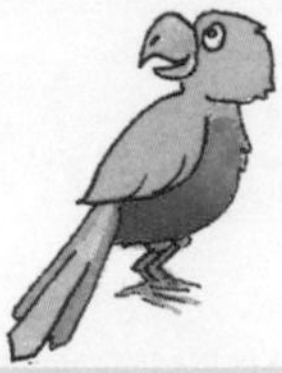

1. Name two 3-D shapes which have 6 faces, 12 edges and 8 vertices.

   ________________ ________________

2. Circle the correct shape. This can of beans is a

   tetrahedron     cylinder     pyramid

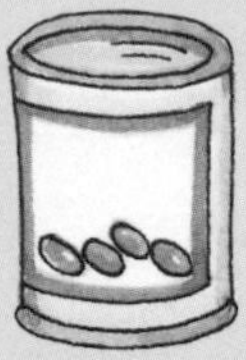

3. How many faces has a triangular prism? ______

4. Name the 3-D shape which has 6 vertices, 6 faces and 10 edges. ________________

5. Increase €8.60 by 50%. ____________

6. Reduce 3kg by 25% ____________

7. Find the cost of this bicycle. ________________

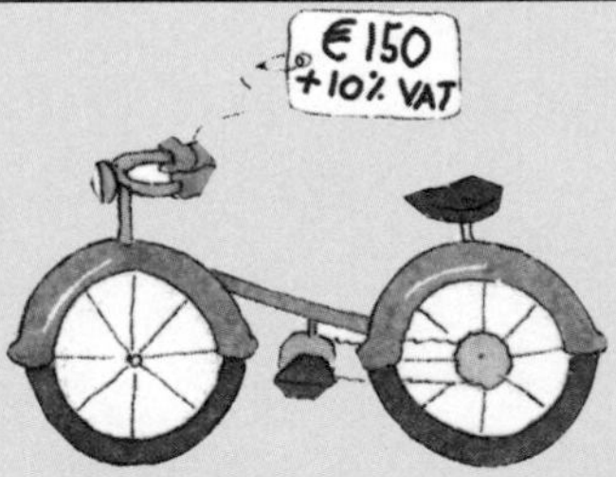

€150
+10% VAT

8. How much would you have to pay for a computer worth €920 if the price was reduced by 20% in a sale? ________________

9. Find the area of this rectangle.

   ________________

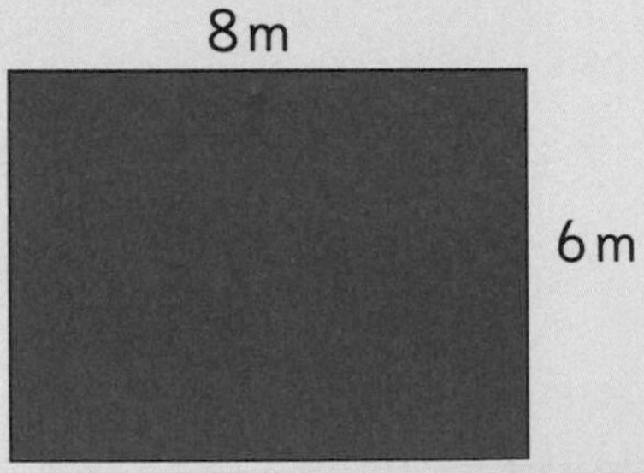

8m
6m

10. One side of a square measures 10m.
    Find the area of the square. ________________

11. What is the area of this garden?

    ________________

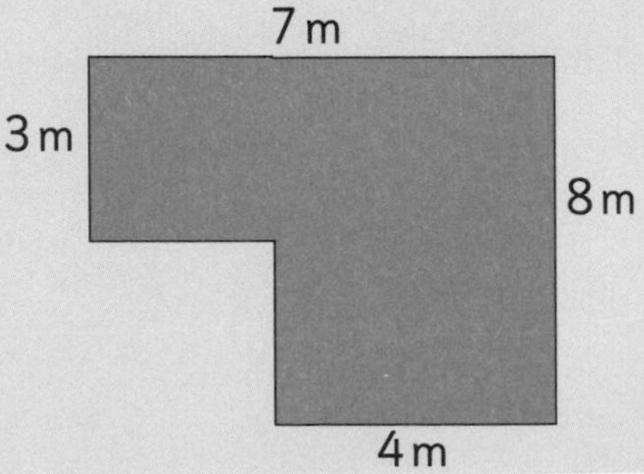

7m
3m
8m
4m

12. It cost €1470 to carpet a rectangular room with this carpet. What was the area of the room? _____

Twenty-four fifth class children were asked to choose their favourite sports. The results of the survey are shown on this pie chart. Look at the chart and answer questions 13 – 16.

13. How many children preferred football? _____

14. How many children preferred basketball? _____

15. How many more children preferred swimming to hurling? _____

16. What percentage of the 24 children preferred football? _____

17. Fill in the missing number. $16$ x $\boxed{\phantom{0}}$ = $112$

18. Fill in the missing symbol. $50$ $\boxed{\phantom{0}}$ $18$ = $32$

19. Write as a number sentence:

Jack shared 28 sweets between himself and his three friends. How many sweets did each child get? _____

20. $7 \times 3 \div 3 + 9 + (10 - 2) =$ _____

How well did you do? Tick the box that shows your score.

| ☐ | ☐ | ☐ | ☐ |
|---|---|---|---|
| 18-20 | 15-17 | 10-14 | 0-9 |
| Excellent | Very Good | Good | Keep up the good work |

# Chapter 32
## A long look back

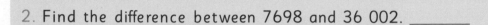

1. Find the sum of these five numbers: 356, 9043, 89, 8 and 15 027. _____

2. Find the difference between 7698 and 36 002. _____

3. The sum of the angles in a triangle = _____

4. Which of these angles is **not** shown here: acute, obtuse, reflex or right angle?

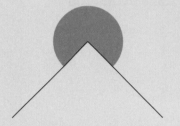   _____

5. Draw a line which is perpendicular to this red line. _____

6. €126.50 ÷ 25 = _____

7. Five of these cakes costs €4.45. How much would 9 cakes cost? _____

8. A newsagent which opens seven days a week sold 8959 newspapers in May. What was the average number of newspapers sold per day in May? _____

9. Is the number which is 9 less than 126, an odd or an even number? _____

10. Circle the square number in this list: 23,   24,   25,   26,   27

11. What fraction of this pizza is missing? _____

12. Fill in the missing number: $\dfrac{3}{5} = \dfrac{}{10}$

13. Add these four numbers: 2.6, 126.125, 1203.75 and 99. _____

14. From 620.75 take 39.825. _____

# A long look back

15. Áine lives 8 km from school and her friend Paul lives 1.75 km closer to the school than Áine. How far is Paul's house from the school? _____

36.175m

16. Find the perimeter of this shape.

_____

27.5m

17. The angle between the hands of this clock measures

_____

18. Measure this angle. _____

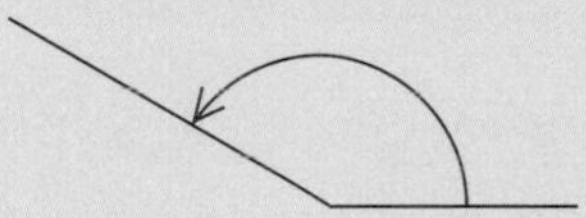

19. If the radius of a circle measures 7 cm, what is the length of the diameter? _____

20. How many **more** sides has a quadrilateral than a triangle? _____

21. Find the missing factors of 24.

__1__ , __2__ , ____ , ____ , ____ , ____ , ____ , __24__

22. Circle the prime number in this list: 42, 43, 44, 45.

23. Write $\frac{18}{4}$ as a mixed number in its simplest form. _____

24. How many bunches of eight flowers can be made from 74 flowers? _____

25. Round 207.603 to the nearest whole number. _____

# A long look back

26. By how much is 7.275 x 8 less than 424.97 ÷ 7? _____

27. Would you use kilogrammes or grammes to measure the weight of a packet of crisps? _____

28. Find the average weight of these three boys: 26.725kg, $30\frac{1}{2}$kg, 20kg 52g. _____

29. This bag contains 10 black and 10 white socks. What is the smallest number of socks you must take out (without looking inside) to be sure to have two socks of the same colour? _____

30. If you roll a dice once, you have a better chance of rolling a 6 than any other number. True or False? _____

31. Write in the next four numbers in this sequence: 6, 4, 2, ___, ___, ___, ___.

32. How many whole numbers are there between negative 2 and positive 5? _____

33. Work out the answers to (a) $2\frac{1}{3} + \frac{3}{4}$ and (b) $4\frac{2}{3} - 1\frac{1}{6}$ and write the bigger answer on this line. _____

34. The Murphy family ordered these two pizzas for dinner.
They each had the following fractions of a pizza:
Dad $\frac{5}{8}$, Mum $\frac{1}{2}$, John $\frac{3}{8}$ and Anne $\frac{1}{4}$.

    How much pizza was left over after the meal? ⬚

35. Write 9.45 p.m. in 24-hour time. _____

36. If a teacher starts work at 08.50 and finishes at 14.30, how many hours and minutes does she work in a full school week? _____

37. 8007ml = _____ l _____ ml = _____ . _____ l

38. Janet bought a 3 litre bottle of water for €2.99. Susan also bought 3 litres of water but she bought the water in 750ml bottles. How much more than Janet did Susan pay for the 3 litres of water? _____

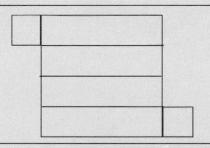

39. Change 90% to a decimal. _____

40. Find 75% of €86.04. _____

41. A tetrahedron is a _____ _____

42. This is a net of a _____

43. Find the full price of this CD player. _____

44. How much would you expect to pay for a computer worth €900 if the price was reduced by 25% in a sale? _____

45. Find the area of this shape. _____

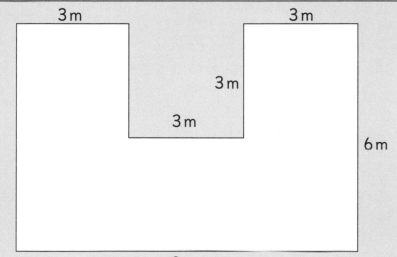

3 m

3 m

3 m

3 m

6 m

9 m

# A long look back

46. This man paid €26 per square metre for paving stones for his patio. If his patio measures 7.5m in length and 6.8m in width, how much did he pay for the paving stones? _____

47.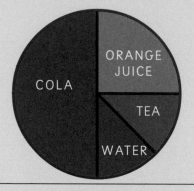

This pie chart shows the favourite drinks of a group of fifth class children. Eight children preferred orange juice. How many children are in the full group? _____

48. Complete this pie chart using the data from this table.

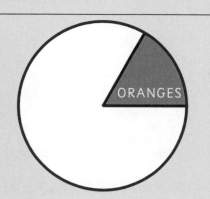

| Children | 12 | 12 | 6 | 6 |
|---|---|---|---|---|
| Favourite fruit | Apple | Banana | Grapes | Orange |

49. Write this word story as a number sentence and then write the answer. Jack shared 45 sweets between himself and his four friends. How many sweets did each child receive? _____

50. $9 \times 4 \div 6 + 9 + (16 - 2) =$ _____

How well did you do? Tick the box that shows your score.

| 45–50 | 35–44 | 25–34 | 0–24 |
|---|---|---|---|
| Excellent | Very Good | Good | Keep up the good work |

# NOTES

# NOTES

# NOTES

# NOTES

# NOTES

# NOTES

# NOTES

# NOTES